I BELIEVE that you have an unexplored talent. My conviction grows stronger every year as I find thousands of people just like you searching to express something. If you have not made a professional career of art I'd like to talk to you all the more.

I BELIEVE that in the life of everyone there comes a time when the Art Spirit is dominant. You may have passed it when you were 5 or 7 or 11 years of age. But it will come again several times in your life when you are looking for something outside your practical everyday routine.

I BELIEVE that you have moments when you drop your cares and wish you could feed that little spark of immortality that needs nourishment from the beauty of the world around you. This universe is full of wonders that few of us see until some part of our brain and soul is reawakened. When we again become aware of "the long reaches of the peaks of song, the rift of dawn, the reddening of the rose," as poet Edwin Markham has so aptly put it.

THIS NEW BOOK is my contribution to you the beginner to help you awaken that hidden talent so you may find happiness and genuine fun in the world around you through the hobby of drawing and painting.

JON GNAGY

Published by
ARTHUR BROWN & BRO., INC.
NEW YORK 19, N. Y.

MATERIALS • You need two carbon pencils, a light gray, a dark gray, and a black chalk. You also need a sandpaper pencil sharpener, a kneaded eraser and a piece of ordinary cleansing tissue.

CARBON PENCILS give the blackest lines you can make without using ink. Carbon pencil technique combines better with chalk than graphite does because it does not shine and graphite does give off a gloss.

(Below) When you want to draw fine, sensitive outlines, give your carbon pencil a SHARP ROUND POINT.

(Below) When you want to make bold lines, use the sandpaper sharpener to give a FLAT CHISEL POINT.

TONE WITH PENCIL • Here are three pencil techniques you can use for laying in tones. By drawing lines side by side with either the round or chisel point, by cross-hatching, or lay your pencil on its side.

TONE WITH STOMP • The paper stomp shown below is a special pencil-like roll of stiff paper with a soft tapered tip. Soft tones may be made with the paper stomp by first grinding some chalk on your sandpaper, then roll the tapered end of the stomp in it and smudge the tone onto your drawing paper.

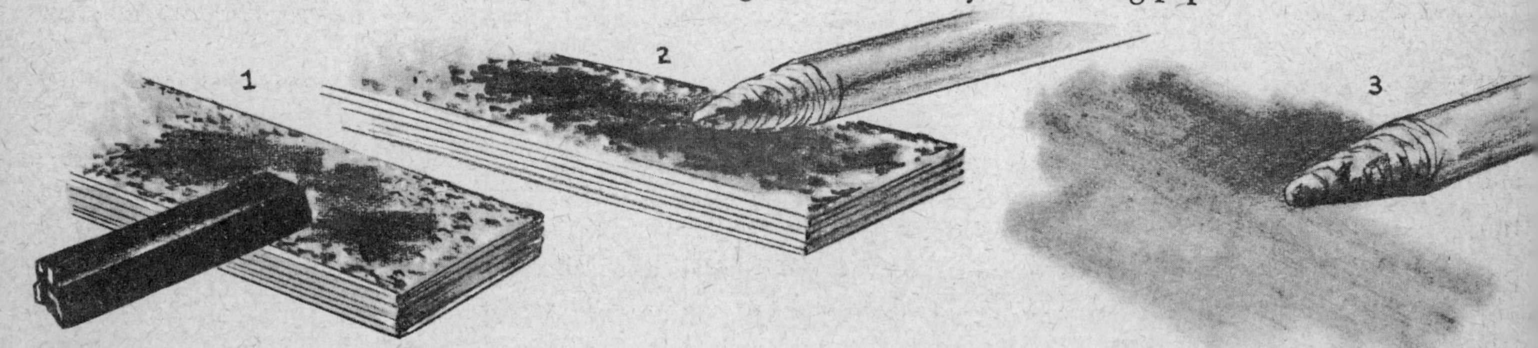

TONE WITH CHALK • Broad sweeping tones can be made quickly by laying a piece of chalk on its side. Softer blending can then be done by going over it with a piece of cleansing tissue or chamois skin or stomp.

WARM-UP EXERCISES

• Every athlete, dancer, singer or performer in any field must practice and practice constantly to achieve success. Just before going on the stage to give a performance every actor does an intense warm-up. He owes it to his audience as well as to his own success to do the best he can, so he goes through his paces. If you expect your hand and pencil to do what you want them to do, be sure to go through these warm-up exercises before doing each drawing lesson.

LINE • ***(Below)*** **1** Practice these lines because they cover every direction of stroke you can make. Starting at the left they are vertical, horizontal, diagonal, simple curves, compound curves, and spirals.

SHAPE • ***(Below)*** **2** When an area is completely surrounded by line it is called shape. Shape has length and width. But line has only length. The basic shapes are the square, circle, triangle and free shapes.

FORM • ***(Below)*** **3** When depth is added to a shape it becomes a FORM, because it has thickness. It then has three dimensions, namely height, width and depth. The four forms below are now called CUBE, BALL, CONE and CYLINDER, because they are no longer just shapes. Every object in nature is made up of combinations of these four basic forms,so the sooner you start looking for them in objects around you, the quicker you'll draw real pictures. In nature you will find distorted variations of the perfect CUBE, BALL, CONE and CYLINDER.

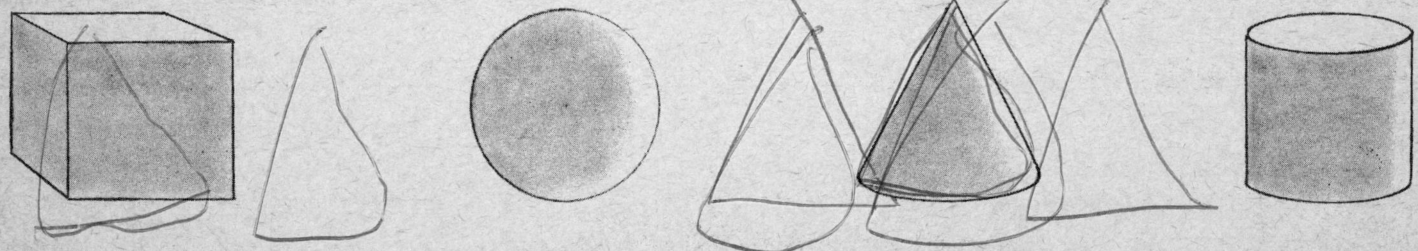

TONE • ***(On the forms above)*** **4** Tone is the overall color of an object. Tone is often referred to as "value." It can be light, medium, or dark in value. In the forms above, the cube, cone and cylinder had an indication of form even before the tone was added, but the ball would ordinarily be called a circle if it were drawn only in outline. In putting the tone on the forms I decided that there would be light shining from the upper right,so a highlight has been left on the top and right of each form. The circle becomes a ball when this highlight occurs.

ON THE NEXT PAGE IS THE SECRET OF REALISTIC DRAWING

SHADING • 5 When light shines on one side of an object, the other side becomes dark. The dark side is shaded. Shading in nature is merely the absence of light, so when you represent a form in a drawing so that it bulges and appears to have thickness, you shade the side away from the light. Shading is the magic touch you give to a picture to make the forms look real. When you sketch objects from nature, sometimes they are not lighted from the best angle to bring out the form,so when you put in the shading be sure that YOU decide where you would put the light if you could move the sun or moon, then you put the shading on the opposite side of each object. In

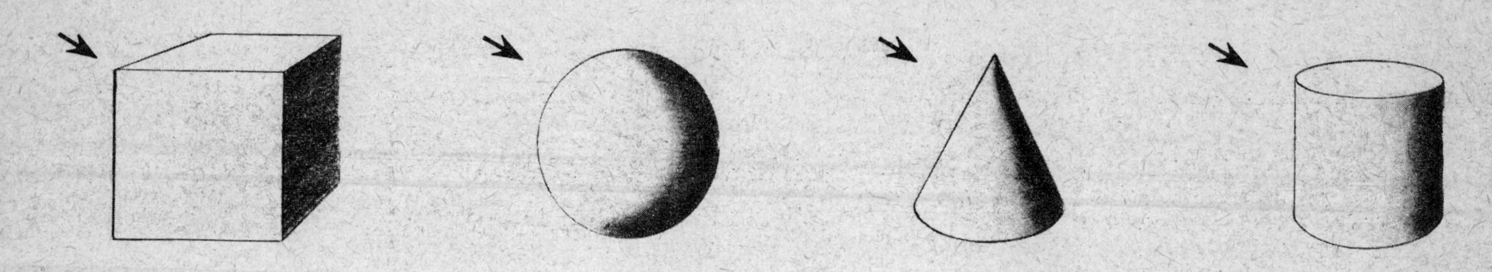

drawing a still life you can control the light. A careful photographer would light his subject to the best advantage and so you, the artist, should do the same thing. For best results in bringing out the form use only a single light instead of having two or more lights. Many lights from different angles wash out each other's shadows, and the object remains flat in appearance. So light your drawing from one direction only.

SHADING IS THE SECRET OF REALISTIC DRAWING

Pay close attention to the way shading blends into tone and gets lighter as it wraps around a rounded surface such as you find on the ball, the cone and the cylinder. You can blend the soft edge very easily with a paper stomp dipped into chalk dust. Give attention to the shapes of shading on each of the basic forms. Notice that the edge of the shading on the cube is sharp and rectangular. Put it in with a pencil.

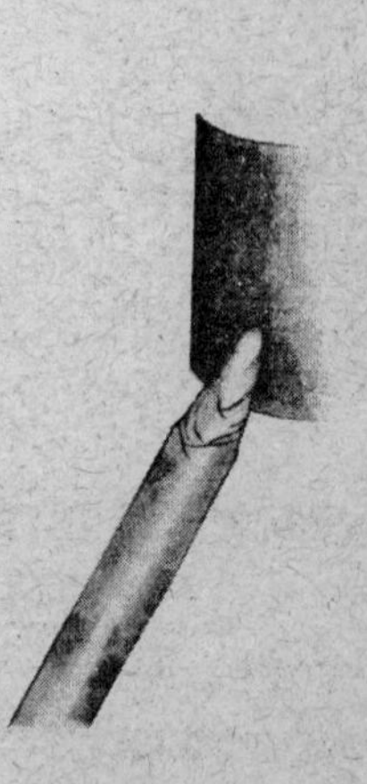

CAST SHADOW • **6** Light shining on an object casts a shadow on another surface. If the other surface is darker than the tone of the object that casts the shadow, you make the cast shadow darker than the shading and vice versa. If a dark tree casts a shadow on snow, the cast shadow should be lighter than the shading on the tree. The shape of the cast shadow is like a vertical cross-section of the object, and it is lying down flat and you are seeing it from the edge,so it looks narrower than the thickness of the object. Make cast shadows lie down by always keeping them very narrow. If you make the cast shadow too thick, it will look as

though it is cut out of paper and is standing on its edge. Take a look at the pages where I show some of the mistakes we make as beginners and you'll see the difference between the right and wrong way to lay a shadow down on the ground or on a table top in realistic drawings. Another very important point to observe about cast shadows is that they often fall across uneven surfaces. If your cast shadow falls on a smooth table top or floor,

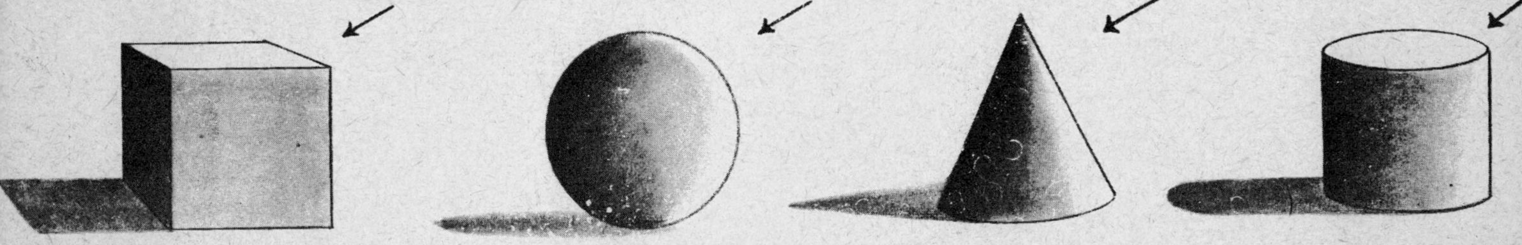

it usually looks pretty straight and regular. But if it goes over rough ground or snow or bumpy objects, it hugs the surface and wraps itself tightly over every bulge and crawls down into crevices instead of stiffly bridging across the valleys. Make your cast shadows *sympathetic* to the surface on which they fall.

TEXTURE • **7** The surface of an object may be described as glossy, smooth, eggshell, bumpy, rough or hilly. These terms and many others are merely approximate attempts to describe texture. The surface quality of an object can be drawn by the artist far more accurately than words can ever portray. If you constantly study textures and practice copying them with pencil, chalk, paper stomp and eraser, you can create wonderful realism in your pictures. Make many close-up studies from nature and discover her secrets.

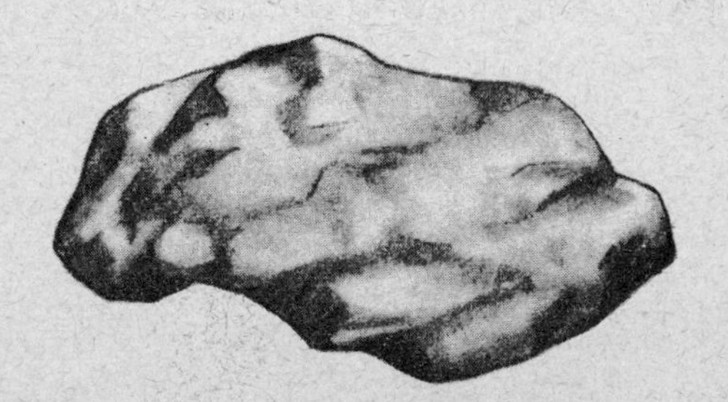

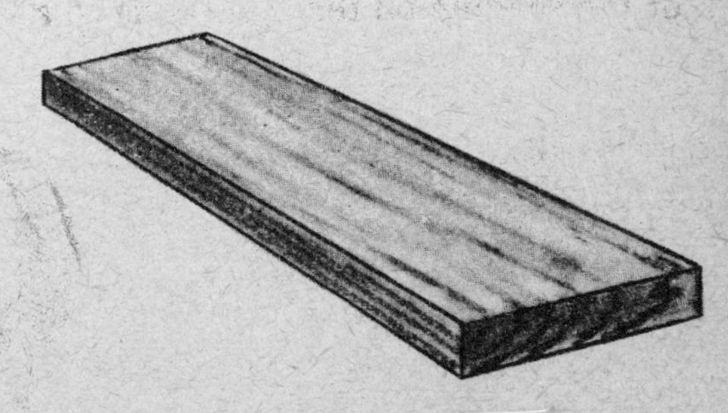

VERY ROUGH BARK **MEDIUM ROUGH STONE** **SMOOTH BOARD**

ON THE NEXT TWO PAGES YOU WILL FIND A REVIEW OF THESE SEVEN BASIC PRINCIPLES AND HOW TO TURN BASIC FORMS INTO FAMILIAR OBJECTS ➡

HOW TO TURN THE BASIC FORMS

INTO SIMPLE FAMILIAR OBJECTS

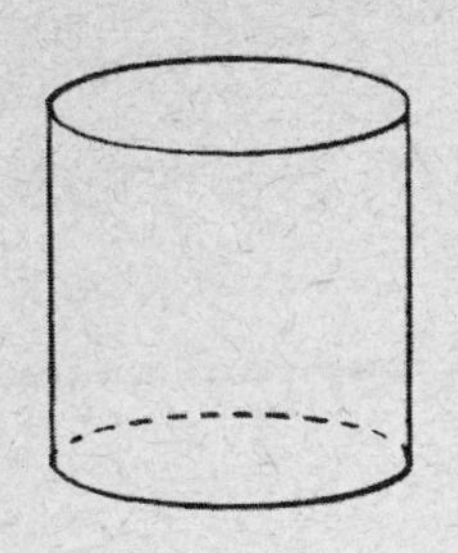

LINE, SHAPE AND FORM • 1, 2, 3—The cube, ball, cone and cylinder here drawn in outline combine line and shape but little form. The ball is not a sphere yet; it is only a circle or flat shape, two-dimensional because it lacks indication of thickness or form. The cube, cone and cylinder however have some appearance of thickness because of perspective in their top and bottom surfaces.

TONE • 4—Tone is the overall color on the entire surface of an object. It may be generally classed as light, medium or dark tone. Applied to the cube, ball, cone and cylinder, the objects begin to have more substance and solidity. Having decided that in this case light shall come from the upper right, a highlight has been left on the top and right edge of each.

SHADING • 5—Shading is drawn where no light falls. Here the light comes from the upper right, so the shading occurs on the opposite side of each object. Now the objects have *form* because they look thick. On the cube the shading is kept sharp and definite at the edge where two planes meet, but on the ball, cone and cylinder the shading should be blended to indicate roundness.

CAST SHADOW • 6—The shadow of a form falling on another surface is the *cast* shadow. The cast shadow is shaped like the object itself, but should be narrowed because it is lying down flat and is seen in perspective. (See pages 10 and 11.) Always make the cast shadow lighter or darker in tone than the shading on the object, to distinguish the object from the shadow it casts.

TEXTURE • 7—Use pencil, chalk and stomp to show different roughness or smoothness characteristic of familiar objects. The grain of wood, weave of fabric, gloss of fruit, or the ridges on a stack of books are all textures that can be reproduced by lines, dots, smudges, etc. To get that final satisfying touch of realism in your pictures, study and draw materials and their surface textures constantly.

VARIATIONS • When you draw familiar objects from nature, always look for variations and combinations of basic forms. For example: a house is made up of cubes and half cubes. A pumpkin is a ball with curved cylinder sections around it, and the stem is a cylinder. The corn shock is a rough cone with a frazzled top. The log is a cylinder foreshortened and has perspective.

ON THE NEXT PAGE YOU MAKE A PICTURE

COMPOSITION

• Don't make dull, static compositions! WHAT MAKES A COMPOSITION DULL? When you make all objects about the same size or you place them where they divide your picture in half. When you have too many straight lines, and when you make everything in the picture the same tone value, you have dull compositions. ***YOU WANT DYNAMIC MOVEMENT*** in your pictures. You want lines, shapes, spaces and tones to have movement. By movement I DON'T MEAN MOTION such as the speed lines of a fellow in a comic strip getting hurled through space. I mean the kind of movement you experience by seeing forms, lines and tones have different sizes, different shapes and different values. I mean variety. A picture should have dynamic movement in order to appeal to your artistic sense. Draw the dynamic composition in the large frame below and turn the basic forms into a corn shock, a pumpkin, a fence post and a house. The curved lines should be smudged and broadened into furrows with corn stubble sticking up in them. This is your ARTISTIC IMAGINATION TEST that will prove whether or not you have ANY TALENT in drawing.

PERSPECTIVE baffles most people. The fact is that we can't see things as they really are. For example, we know that the edges of a road are parallel, and that they don't come together in the distance, but if you look down a long avenue lined with trees of equal size that stretch far away from you, they seem to converge at a vanishing point. The real reason is that the back of your eye is a screen like the film in your camera, and it makes close images look large and distant images look small. So if you are going to draw a convincing

ONE POINT PERSPECTIVE

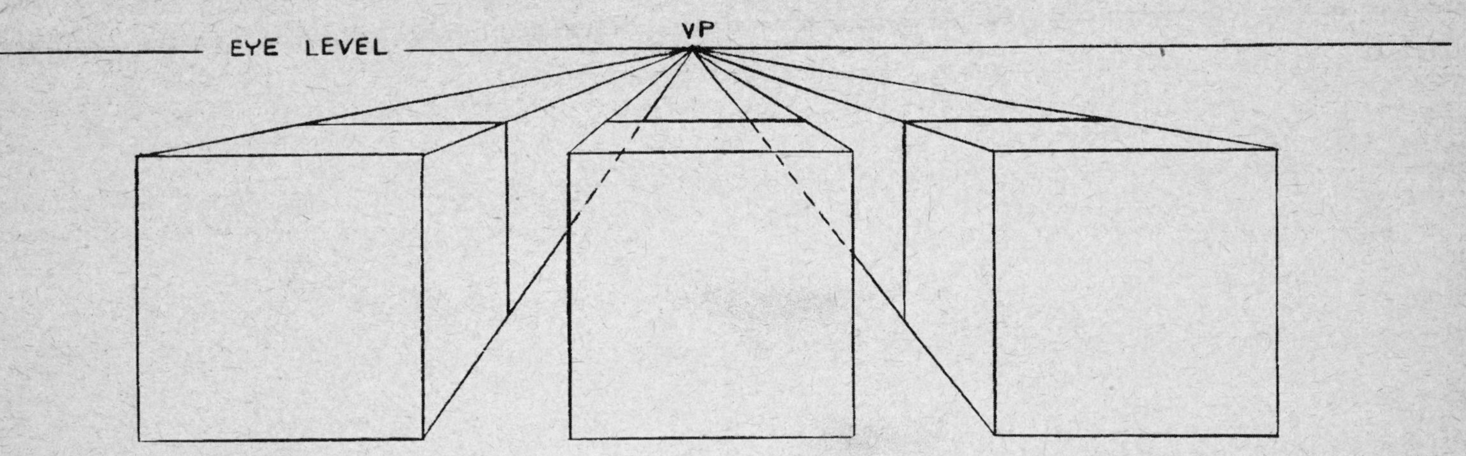

picture as the eye sees it, you must duplicate its impression by making everything in the distance get very small and objects up close must fill the width of the screen. If you are looking at the flat end surface of a cube, you

TWO POINT PERSPECTIVE

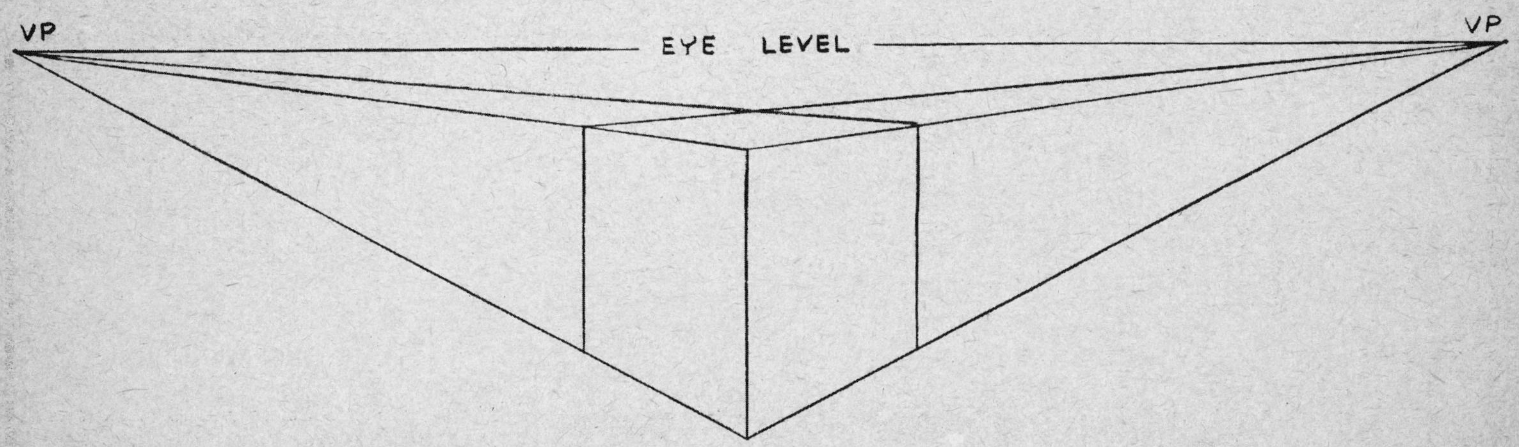

use only one vanishing point. If the corner edge of a cube is closest to you, then you can see both flat planes and they must each have a vanishing point far off beyond both sides of your vision. When you look along a curved road, there are actually hundreds of vanishing points because each change of degree in the curve has its own perspective. The only thing they have in common is that they are all on the same eye level line.

PERSPECTIVE IN A CURVED ROAD

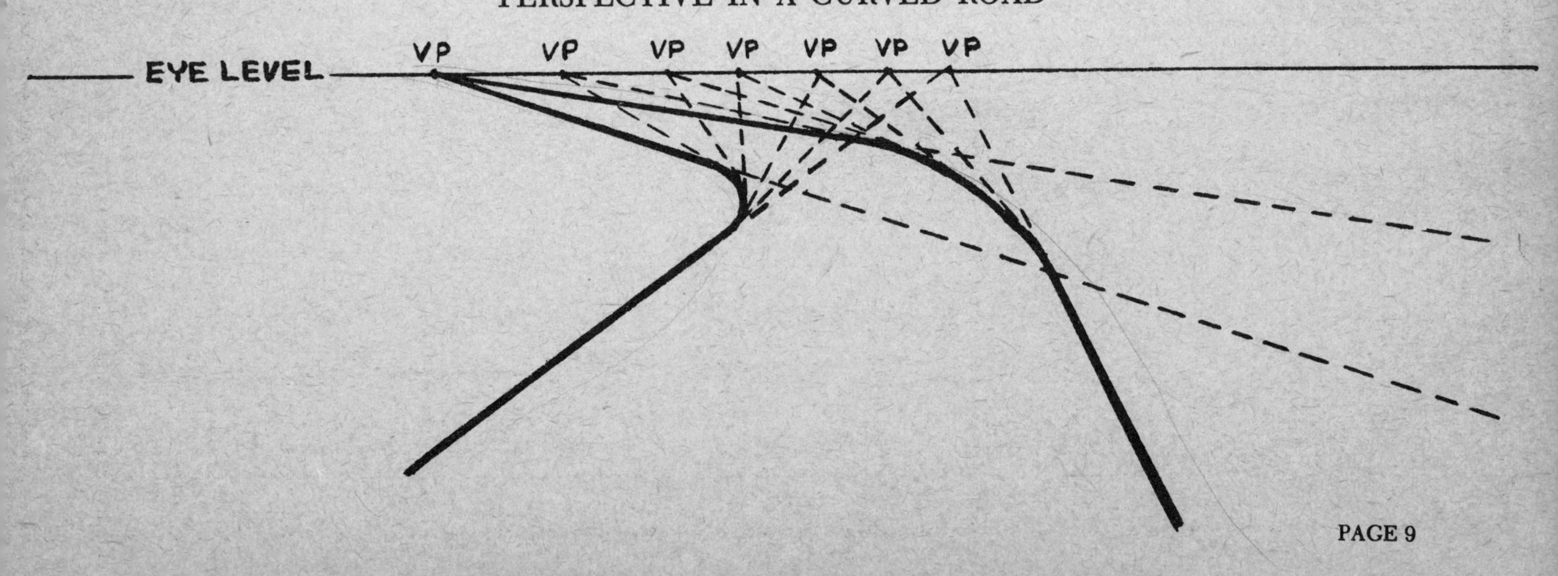

YOU CAN AVOID THESE MISTAKES FROM THE VERY

PRIMITIVE

THIS drawing was not made by a child nor by a primitive grandma or grandpa. I made this drawing myself and put into it the mistakes made by people who want to draw realistically but say they can't. Mistakes that the average sophisticated person says he is ashamed to make. I am not poking fun at this kind of picture because I love this type of naïve drawing when it is done by a child or an untutored sincere adult. I collect such pictures because they *are* sincere impressions of someone's experience. When a picture like this one has been created with true pride and the artist himself feels that he has expressed the spirit of the scene we accept it as a primitive, and love it for its naïve errors— — — — — — —

← *This poor little LAKE is standing on its side—But if you want it to*

These MOUNTAINS → are excellent abstract symbols—BUT you might

← *This PINE TREE looks as though it were cut out of paper and pasted to the mountain side,*

The TREE STUMP → and the BOAT → are fourth-dimensional because you are seeing them

This HOUSE → that Jack built was just a flat stage setting and it got sawed off at one end,

← *This ROAD around the lake was drawn from memory and I remember that it was as wide at the other*

Speaking of TREES, here is one → that has a wider trunk and branches at the top

The BRANCHES of this tree → are barely pasted onto the trunk and might

The CAST SHADOW of this → tree is standing on its side, and it is as wide

START IF YOU WANT TO DRAW REAL PICTURES

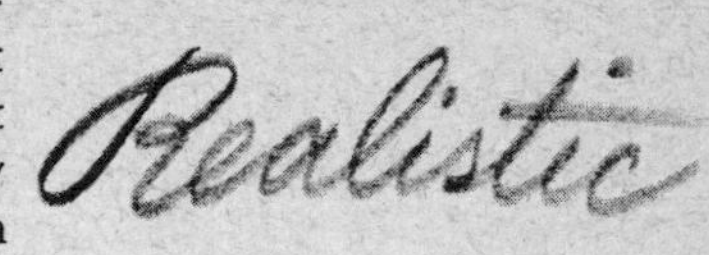

BUT when a person comes to my drawing and painting classes because he wants to make photographically real pictures I know that he doesn't want to be a primitive. Frankly, it would be a sin on my part to try to make a primitive out of him or her, because turning back to imitate something that you are not is obviously false. When you have set yourself the task of drawing realistically I want to show you how you can enjoy doing it more quickly and with the least possible effort. I want to show you how you can avoid the mistakes that you don't want to make. You who are not satisfied until you can draw a picture that is realistic need instruction, whereas the primitive does it and is happy with his results.

ie down flat like this → you may rest easier. Now it won't spill all of its water.

verlap them and make them less steep like this → and they will be more believable.

ut if you want it to look more real, you might make it less regular, and then tone it and shade it like this →

from above and the side all at the same time, but this → is how a camera would see them.

ut when Jack went back to nature he built himself a three-dimensional house →

nd as it was at the beginning, but it looks like this → from where we stand now.

han at the bottom, but this one → is narrower at the top than at the bottom of the trunk.

nap off, but these branches → grow out of the trunk and are actually a part of it.

s the tree, but this tree SHADOW hugs the ground and looks narrow and flat.

NOW YOU ARE READY TO DRAW REAL PICTURES →

HARVEST

A simple lesson for beginners based chiefly on the ball form

1 Start your outlines light and sketchy. Draw the circles for the fruits and vegetables with a carbon pencil. The closer the object to the foreground, the lower you should place it in the frame of your picture. Draw the pear with a small ball form and large ball form connected by an outline. After you have drawn the circles, draw the line for the table top a little below the one-third mark in the picture frame.

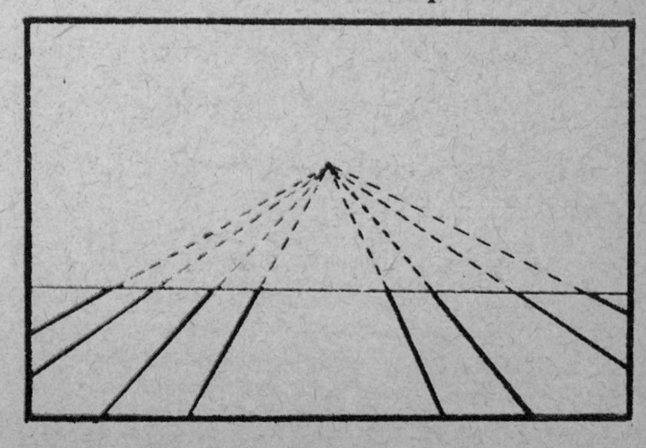

The paper stomp is a handy tool of many uses. It is merely a roll of special paper, specially made to absorb charcoal, crayon, graphite, chalk or pastel. First put some chalk on the sandpaper pad, then roll the tapered tip of the stomp into the dust on the sand-pad. Then use the stomp as you would use a sharpened pencil on its side. To shade the opening in the apple simply make a single curved stroke as indicated in the close-up sketch.

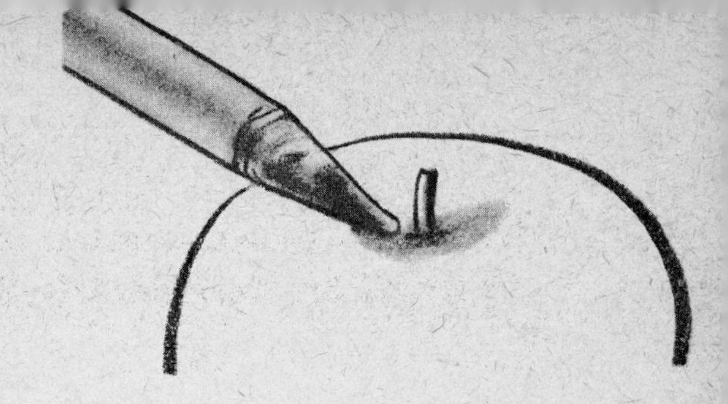

2 Draw the shapes of the ears of corn. They are cylinders tapering to cones at the ends. The pumpkin stem is a cylinder. Set it into the top of the ball. Now draw the segments of pumpkin and melon. Use the paper stomp for the melon segments which are not as sharp nor deep as the pumpkin's. Draw a curved line in the top of each apple with the stomp for the cone-like opening into which you draw the stem. Each stem is a cylinder, drawn with the carbon pencil. Place a dot in the very center of the picture as a vanishing point. Use a ruler or the edge of a book to draw the crevices of the boards converging toward that single vanishing point. Random width boards make the areas more interesting.

The kneaded eraser should be molded, pinched and kneaded in your fingers before attempting to use it. If it is not kneaded and warmed up before using, you'll find that it doesn't work much better than an ordinary eraser. When properly kneaded before using it each time, you'll find that it cleans up smudges, makes highlights, erases lines and even cleans your finger-tips with amazing efficiency. Even after it has gotten black from use, it will work well if kneaded before using it.

3 Draw the corn husks each a little different in size. Wave the lines for a rough irregular effect. With a kneaded eraser, remove the lines that show through the pumpkin stem, apples, corn husks and the circles in the pear. Draw parallel rows of corn on each ear. Break your large light gray chalk into three pieces and use a short piece to tone in the background of the picture. Lay the chalk on its side when using it to cover a broad area and smooth the surface. When the background is all covered, blend it with the paper stomp. Now let's choose the direction of our light. This decision is always up to the person drawing the picture. So let's make the light come from the upper left. This means then that all the shading and cast shadows will be on the right and underside of each object. Use the stomp for shading the right side of the corn husks.

The square chalks can do wonders for you in making large masses of tone with very little effort. You should have a light gray, a dark gray and a very black chalk crayon. Before using the chalks each one should be broken into two or three pieces for best results. Lay the piece flat and press it in the center when you want to make an overall even tone. If you want to make a graduated tone, give the chalk more pressure at one end.

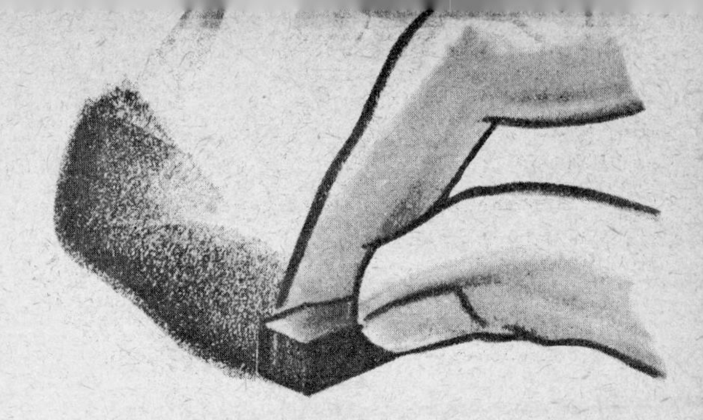

4

The kernels of the corn are small ovals within the parallel lines of the rows. Use the dark gray chalk on its side for toning and shading the stones on the background wall. Turn your drawing sideways and hold the small piece of chalk so that you can give it more pressure at one end. This will help to get the effect of shading on the side of an irregular ball-like form. In this case, shading is on the right and underside of each bulging stone. Draw the wood grain in each board with the corner of the light gray chalk, wiggling it to get variation. Converge the grain of the wood toward the vanishing point. A good look at some actual boards in which the graining is very clear will help you.

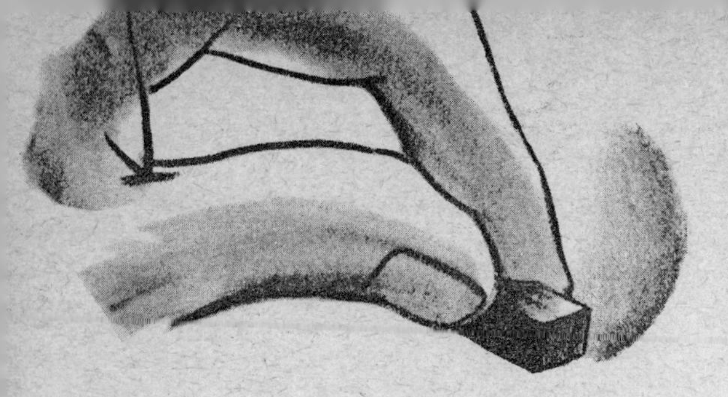

The gray and black chalks can be used with single stroke efficiency for shading the sides of the ball forms of fruit such as the apples, pear, melon and pumpkin. First, practice using the chalk flat to make broad curved strokes. Then do the same thing by pressing closer to one end of the chalk as you make the curved stroke. After a little practice, you'll be toning and shading entire objects in a single stroke. Soon your drawings will have a professional look.

5 Use the carbon pencil to doodle an irregular outline around each stone mass. Turn your drawing upside down if you are right handed, so that you can use the gray chalk for quick shading on the right side of each ball form of fruit, putting the pressure on the point of the chalk but allowing a broad tone that is darker at the one edge and gets lighter toward the opposite end of the chalk. If you are left handed you need not turn the drawing around. After you have shaded the side and undersurface of each form, use the paper stomp to blend and soften the tone at the edge of the shadings and use the stomp to give a little texture to the melon. Shade each kernel of corn with the point of the stomp. With the pencil, cast shadows on the kernels under the edges of the husks, shade the pumpkin stem and give it a stringy texture.

Try as often as possible to make your cast shadows transparent. By transparent I mean you can see several dark and medium dark tones in the shadow instead of its looking jet black. In the sketch at the right you can see the darker grain of the wood become even darker where it passes through the cast shadow of the pear. This effect of transparent shadows can be gotten by keeping the cast shadow light enough so you can still put darker strokes in it.

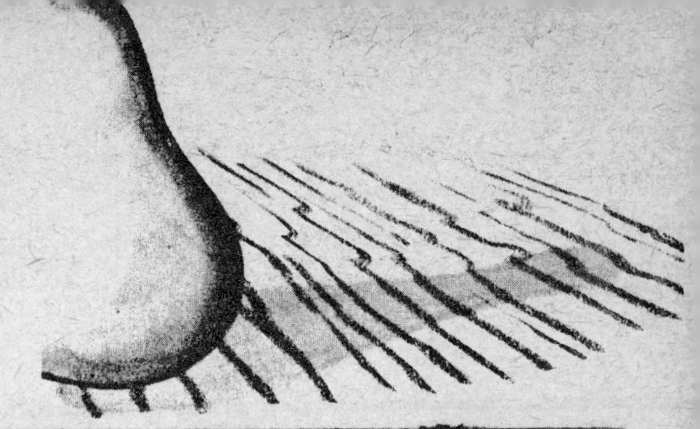

6 With the carbon pencil cast shadows from the corn, following the contour of the bulging stones in the background. Cast the pumpkin shadow across part of the wall. Cast the shadow of the melon, apples, pear, and pumpkin on the table top. Extend the pear shadow long and narrow. Most of these shadows are elliptical. Cast a shadow on top of the pumpkin from the small cylinder form of the stem. Use the carbon pencil also to put lines of rough texture on the corn husks and flecks of coloring on the apple, pear, pumpkin stem and stones. Cross-hatch and irregular strokes will help give roughness to the stones. Also, break up the edges of the stones with a few irregular marks. Put dark accents on the shaded side of each object with the black chalk and fuse together the tone of the stones in the background with the stomp.

MISSISSIPPI STEAMBOAT

An easy exercise in drawing still life, figures and action

1 Draw a horizontal line for the distant shore of the river at a point a little less than one-third down from the top of your paper. Draw another line for the dock at a point about one-third up from the bottom of the paper. Draw a cylinder in the position shown. Use the light gray chalk on its side for toning in the sky, pressing very lightly. Blend with a piece of cleansing tissue, or chamois skin, for a lighter tone. Indicate the far bank and trees with the light gray chalk and put in a reflection with the small stomp rubbed in gray chalk. Draw several light gray streaks horizontally through the center of the river and spread them out with tissue and the stomp.

An ellipse is a circle that is lying down and you are seeing it from an edge view. As when you look at the top of a drinking glass or a barrel. Therefore, you are seeing it in perspective instead of from a bird's eye view. Practice making flat ellipses by free arm movement and always reverse the stroke. After going around the ellipse one way, go back over it the other direction as indicated in the warm-up exercises back on page 3.

2 For bales of cotton on the dock draw one square on top of another, rounding off the corners. Locate a vanishing point in the center of the page on the horizon line. From that point draw the edges of the cube-like forms for the bales and add the line to the far end of each cube, rounding the corners off those also, and adding a third bale on top. In the right foreground draw the elliptical tops of two kegs and curve the sides. Draw a foreshortened molasses barrel to the left of the bales. It is a front view of a circle with edges of a cylinder converging to the same vanishing point used for the cotton bales. Indicate a steel band around the piling and draw another piling beyond the edge of the dock. Draw some oval-shaped bags of rice in the left hand corner and add little ears to a couple of the bags. From the vanishing point draw the boards in perspective. Use a ruler to get the lines straight.

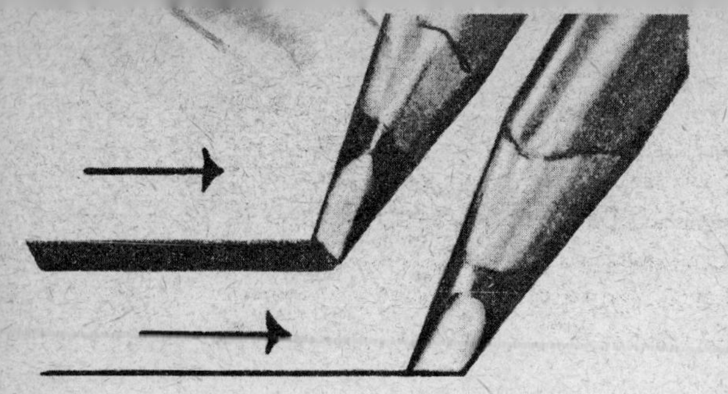

If you take the time to prepare your pencils with a chisel point, you'll find that they work for you with much less effort on your part. The best pencil sharpener for you is a draughtsman's pencil sharpener that makes a long blunt point. If you don't have a draughtsman's sharpener, use a razor blade or very sharp knife to get a long lead. Then sandpaper the sides of the lead to make a flat chisel end so you can make thick or thin lines.

3 Draw a long rectangular shape for the body of the boat, overlapping river and horizon. Draw the long line of the gunwale, turning it up a little in front. Draw a half circle or upside down U shape for the housing of the side-wheel, and on top a small, long cube. For a woman on the landing draw a triangle for shoulders and back and an upside down cone for the skirt, ovals for mutton-leg sleeves, curved cones for arms, a small triangular shape for collar, a circle for the back of the bonnet and another circle for the hood, partially overlapped. Indicate the boy's body structure with a large X. Draw his arms and shoulders with one bold stroke and locate his head with a circle. Wrap hoops around the barrels and connect the pilings with a chain, then erase any line that shows through the solid object in front of it.

To get the best results from your kneaded eraser, learn to mold and pinch it to a point or flat chisel-like edge. Do this after each stroke while using it because each stroke blunts the edge of the eraser. When you want to pick out a highlight or erase in a small corner-like area, take the time to prepare the edge of the eraser constantly. You can get a white straight line by erasing along the edge of a piece of paper.

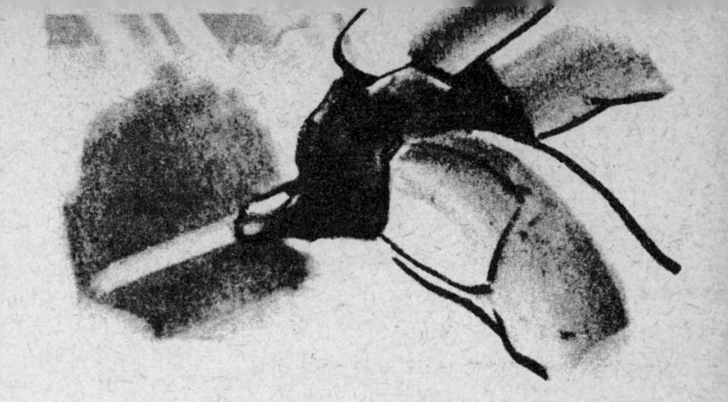

4 Deciding that the light comes from the upper right in this case, use the dark gray chalk to shade the left side of the cube-like bales of cotton, cylinder forms of barrels and pilings, oval bags of rice, and the woman's form. Curve the shadows on her skirt and shade the right sleeve underneath. With the carbon pencil draw the boy in silhouette shaded by the woman. Thicken his limbs, and indicate waving fingers. Draw a tapered square for his body. Connect the head to shoulders and indicate a broad-brimmed hat with a squarish crown. Use the carbon pencil to shade the barrels and the right hand inside rims of those standing. Pinch the kneaded eraser to a point to remove the tones of the far shore within the boat.

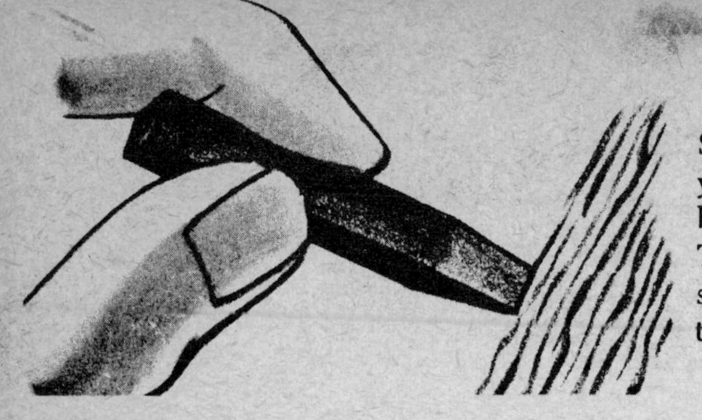

Sharpen the chalks on the sandpaper pad to make a chisel-like end on each. Then you can use them edgewise or broadside to get a variable stroke. Wood grain can be easily indicated by wavering the angle of the chalk as you stroke along edgewise. This kind of motion creates a thick and thin width to the wood grain strokes. Collect some actual boards that have clearly defined wood graining and then practice imitating their patterns as accurately as you possibly can.

5 With the paper stomp tone in the boat lighter than the horizon. Draw the hull of the boat beneath the gunwale with the light gray chalk. With the carbon pencil draw the details of the posts, smokestacks, flags, windows and passengers. Tone in the top surfaces of the cotton bales and landing surface with the light gray chalk. Lightly shade the irregular squares on the end of each cotton bale. Shade the left and under side of each. Later the rope bindings will be drawn. Put in the barrel stays with a light gray tone throughout the middle sections, leaving a highlight on the right side of each form. Tone in the barrel ends, middle areas of the rice bags, pilings, woman's form, bonnet, cape and skirt. If the end of your chalk is too blunt, sharpen it to a chisel point on the sandpaper card and blend the rounded surfaces with the small paper stomp dipped into gray chalk from the sandpaper pad.

Deposit some gray and black chalk on a sandpaper pad so you have two or three tones of chalk dust to dip the stomp into. Roll the tapered tip of the stomp into the light chalk dust first. When you scribble it onto the paper to make smoke, try rolling the stomp in your fingers to get some of the accidental twirls and twists of real smoke. Then repeat the same thing by dipping into darker gray. The black accents should be added last.

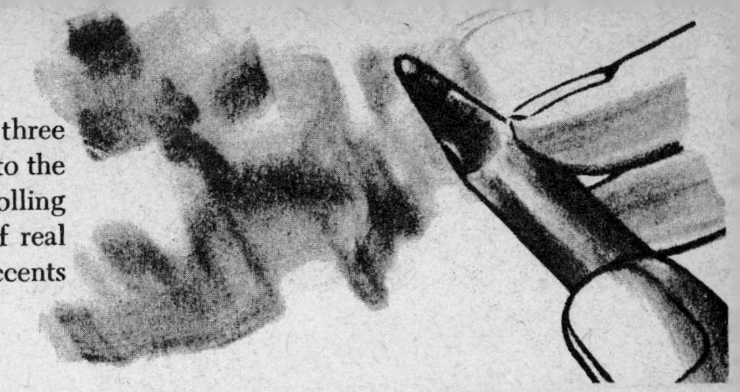

6 Draw the shapes of the cast shadows from the cotton bales, the barrel lying down, the piling and the woman's dress. Make the shadows lie down and then fill in by stroking the surface with the pencil in the direction of the grain of the boards. Draw the ropes around the cotton with the carbon pencil and make them press between the square segments of bulging cotton. Draw the smoke from the boat with the dark gray chalk and the reflections of boat and smoke with the paper stomp dipped in gray chalk. Draw the seams and marking on the bags, more grain in the wood and other final touches with the carbon pencil.

RFD AMERICA

A study in creating depth with contrasting sizes of objects

1 Draw the roadway and the distant hill in light outline with the carbon pencil. At the far end of the roadway, draw a cube with sharp perspective in one side converging toward point x. Draw a square to the right side to make a section of a building. Slant the bottom edges of the building to follow the slopes of the hill. With the paper stomp rubbed in gray chalk, draw ruts in the snow. Keep them narrow in the distance and wider in the foreground. Let's have the light come from the upper right, so tone the left slope of the hill on which the house sits.

In toning and shading the edge of a snow bank, start with the lightest gray chalk. Put more pressure on one end of the chalk so that you automatically get the soft blended effect of the rounded snow forms. If both edges of the stroke remain sharp, it won't look like snow. You can also use a clean stomp and cleansing tissue for softening the blended surface even more. Remember the tone should blend from gray to pure white. Practice on a separate sheet.

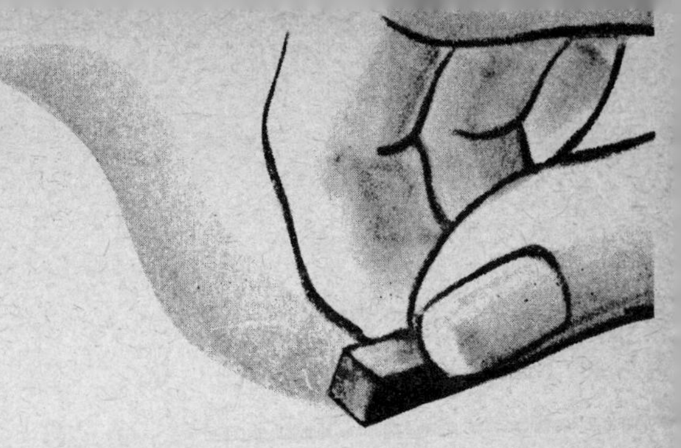

2 Draw a triangular shape at the top of the front plane of the cube to make the end of the building roof. Draw the thick blanket of snow on top of this. Add a roof to the other section. Use the paper stomp dipped in light gray chalk for some shading on the left side of the roof and the underside of the overhanging eave. Use the same gray chalk for toning the left side of the distant hill. Draw the cube form of the chimney with the pencil and make a dark accent under each eave. Tone the side of the road that turns away from the light by placing the chalk on its side and exert more pressure on one end of it. Blend the right edge of the road softly with cleansing tissue. Use the stomp in gray chalk to cast a shadow on the right hand ditch and soften the line of the opposite ditch.

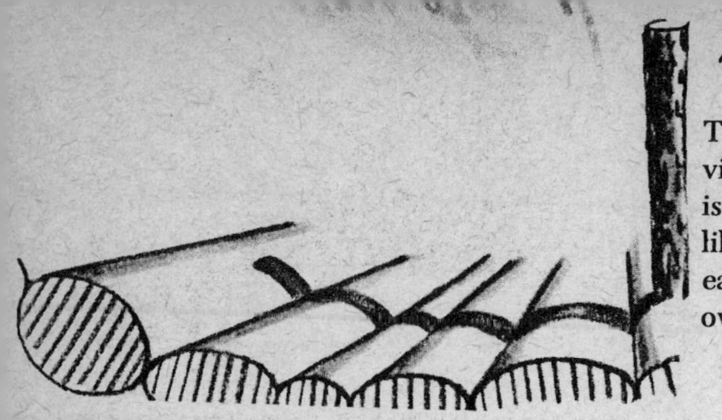

The cast shadow across the snow bank and the ruts of the road can be very convincing if you bear in mind one important principle. The main thing to remember is that the cast shadow hugs the surface of the forms, and these forms are very much like a group of cylinders lying side by side. So wrap your strokes part way around each form and make them drop down into the crevices and then curve them up over the bulge of each ridge.

3 Shade the left side of the building with the dark gray chalk. Trim the end of the chalk to a small chisel point on the sandpaper. See small sketch above. With the dark gray chalk cast a shadow from the building, following down the slope, across the road and into the ruts. Draw the boards on the front surfaces of the building with the light gray chalk. Draw the rectangular windows and doors then put another dark accent under the eaves with the carbon pencil. With the dark gray chalk cast the tree shadows across the front of the picture, down the slope into the ruts and up the opposite slope, each stroke growing narrower toward the left. Also make a broad cast shadow across the front of the picture. Blend with the tip of the paper stomp and darken the ruts in the shadow with a pencil. Draw several pine trees beyond the house, starting with vertical lines and sloping the branches down in shaggy, triangular shapes.

Before toning in the overall sky it is important to bring the tone along the edge of the objects that meet the sky. A square chalk held tightly between the thumb and forefinger can be used to start the sky tone with a clean sharp edge. Give more pressure toward the one end of the chalk as shown in the accompanying sketch. After the entire edge is cleanly defined, then you may tone the remainder of the sky by holding the chalk in its middle.

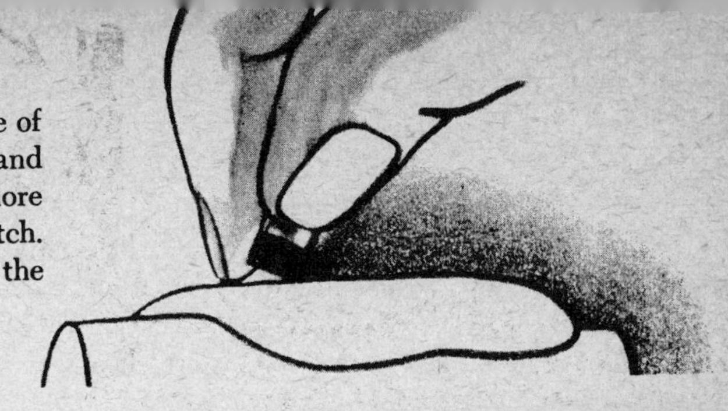

4 Start the mailbox by drawing a long cube form over-lapping the hills and sky. Round off the top of the box like a loaf of bread and put a small irregular blanket of snow on top by drawing an outline with the carbon pencil. Draw a rectangular cube for the board that the box rests on. Keep it flat by showing the edge but very little of the top surface. The post is a cylinder form but at this stage just outline the two edges. Tone in the sky just above the mailbox with a short piece of the light gray chalk laid on its side and lightly follow the outline at the top of the box and the hill. Draw the hedge at the left with the carbon pencil, making it appear to be a long curved cube, following the contour of the hill. Soften the edges of the snow blanket on the hedge with the paper stomp.

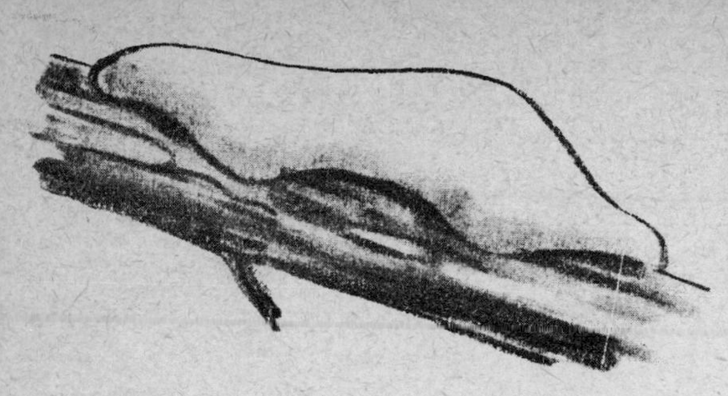

The best way to get the effect of a mound of snow resting on top of an object is to draw the object in outline, then draw the marshmallow-like form of the snow. Make it hug the form. Then tone the object that the snow is resting on. Use the paper stomp dipped in light gray chalk and tone the under edges of the lump of snow to get the effect of roundness. Tuck the cast shadow under the edges with a pencil.

5 With the light gray chalk on its side, finish toning the sky, pressing heavier at the top and left of the sky for an overcast feeling. Draw the stems of the hedge with the carbon pencil. Erase the lines of the hill that show through the mailbox with a kneaded eraser. Tone the front of the mailbox with the light and the dark gray chalk. Draw an irregular edge with the pencil on the board beneath the box to indicate the snow blanket. Use the kneaded eraser to remove the outlines showing through the snow and raise the snow part way up from the platform against the edge of the mailbox. Tone the board light gray, erase the tree shadows from inside the post and tone it with the light gray chalk, leaving a highlight along the right side. Shade the left end of the box with carbon pencil.

Here's the secret for making footprints in the deep snow. Dab the paper stomp into some light gray chalk and start right close in the foreground with the biggest dents. Give the stomp a slight twirl on each footprint to get the effect of a depression. Don't refill the stomp but keep on going back into the picture, making each print smaller and more faint in tone. Refill the stomp with a darker gray and put another dab in the bottom of each dent.

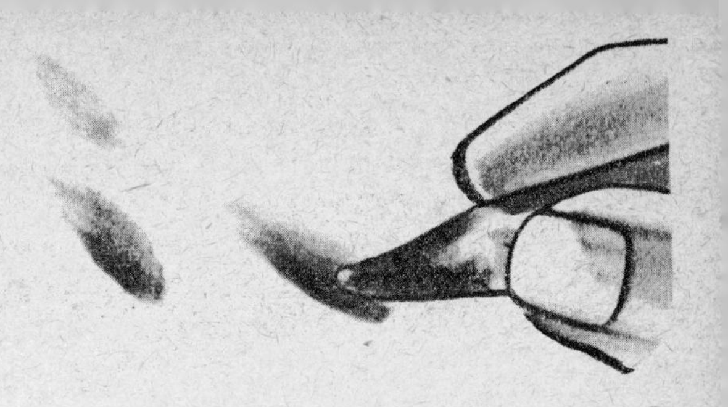

6 Cast a light shadow from the mailbox on the platform with the carbon pencil and small shadows under the snow on both the top of the box and the platform. Indicate some wood grain on the platform edge. Shade the left side of the post with the black chalk and with the carbon pencil indicate texture on the post. Cast the shadow from the platform part way down on the post. Add thickness to the snow on box and board by shading with the paper stomp dipped in light gray chalk. Outline the ends of the box heavily. Draw and tone the flag with the carbon pencil. With the paper stomp draw the smoke and dab in the footprints, making them larger as they come forward. Draw triangular blobs one over the other for two more pine trees, shading the left and under side of each with the carbon pencil. Put snow on the distant trees and draw the weeds in foreground.

THE HARLEQUIN DANE

The aristocrat of dogs. A lesson in black and white contrasts

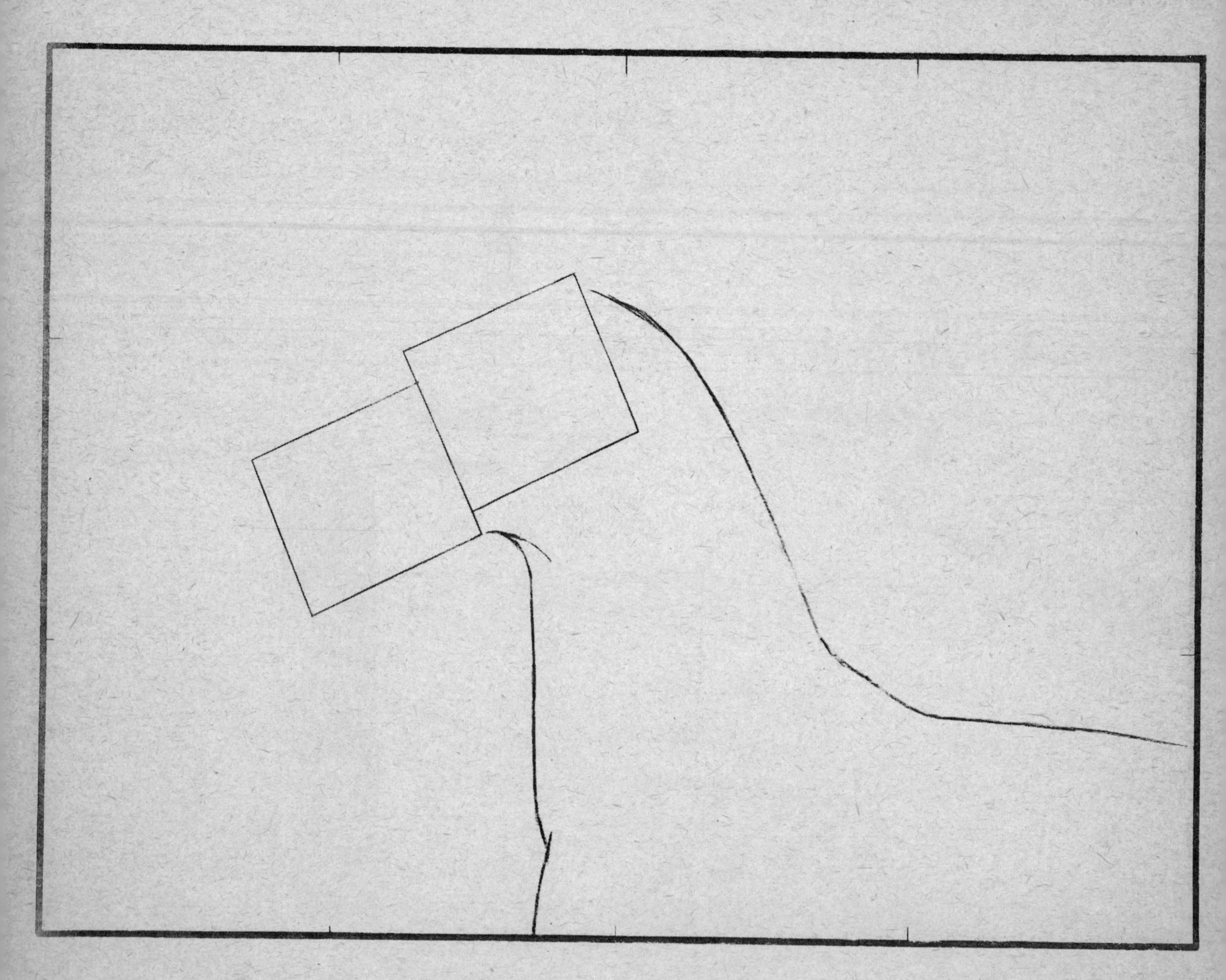

1 Draw two rectangles very lightly, almost but not quite squares; make them a little longer than high, placing them end to end, one slightly offset against the other, and both on the same slant. Draw a curved cylinder form to represent the dog's neck, tapering it wider at the shoulders. Follow the contour of the back lines very carefully and join the head as accurately as possible because the alert gesture of the entire dog will make him look every inch a champion.

The professional method for enlarging a picture is to draw parallel lines vertically and horizontally as shown in the sketch at the right. This way of enlarging may be used whenever you want an exact enlargement. In drawing the Great Dane it is very important to have the exact proportions, so place the cigar box squares and gesture of neck, shoulders and ears as accurately as possible before finishing any detail. Two or three practice attempts are recommended before adding the eyes, mouth, nostrils and tone.

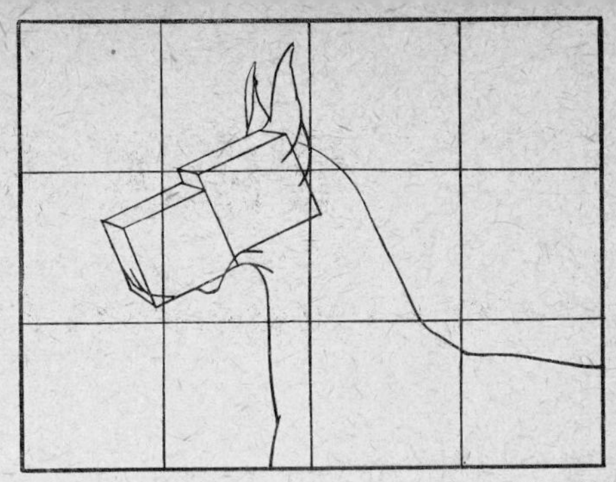

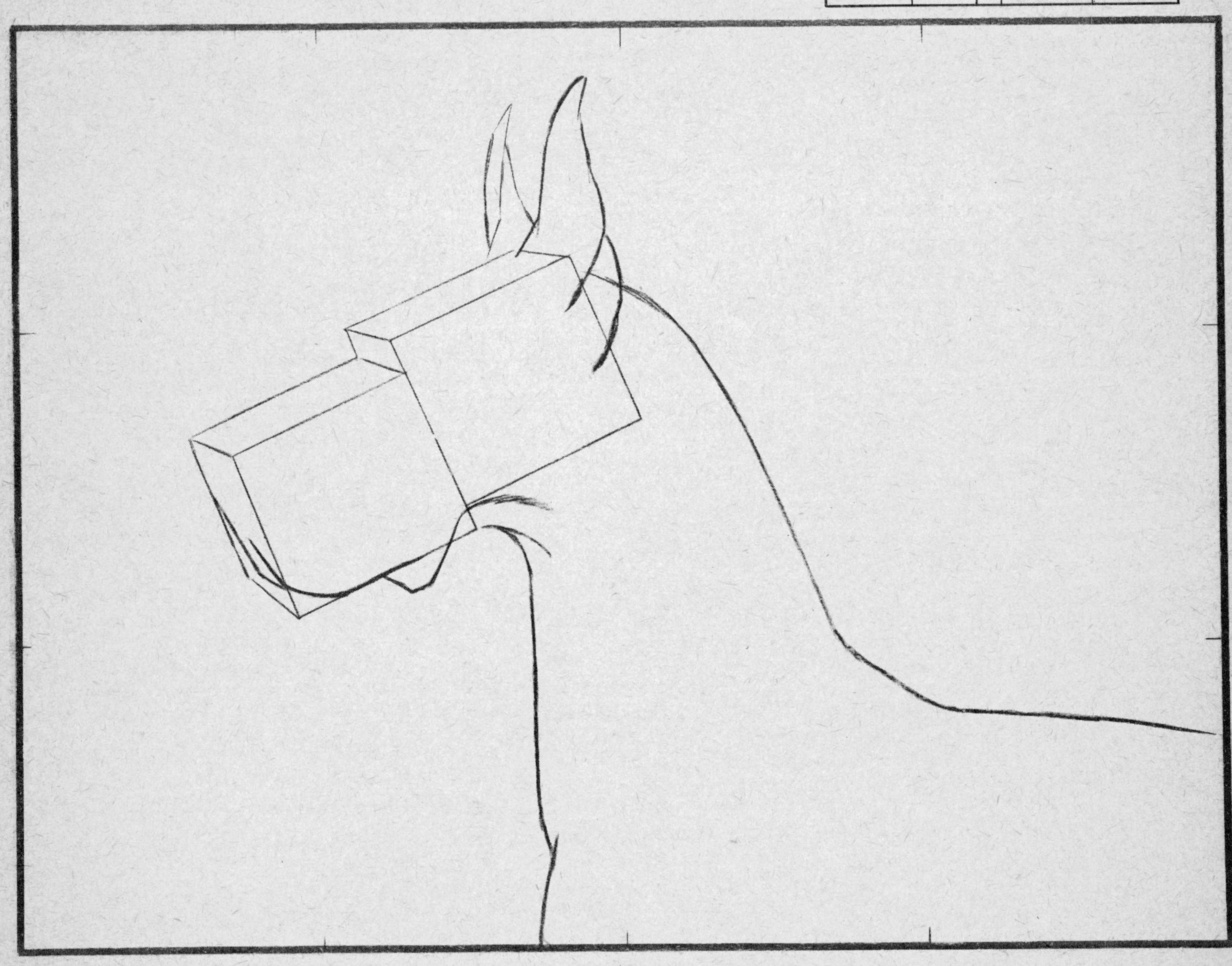

2 Add third dimension by making cube-like forms of the squarish shapes, so that they resemble two cigar boxes. Taper the cone forms of the ears and tilt them carefully. Use the same care in drawing the lip. The split of the lip should come up only half way on the muzzle. Be sure that the loose lower flap of skin from the mouth extends below the cigar box and then curves up to cut off the corner of the box. End the stroke under his jaw in a soft fuzzy line to help make one form melt into another.

The eye is a ball form set deep into an opening in the bony skull. You see only the front of the ball and it has a circular iris that shows a dark circular pupil inside of it. In this view you are seeing the circular iris in perspective so it looks like an ellipse with a smaller ellipse inside. The lids of the eye are flaps that hold the eye ball in the head and they cover the upper part of the iris.

3 The eye sits on a horizontal plane between the two cubes. Make a curved stroke through the corner of the cube for the bone prominence above the eye. The line of the forehead and the top of the muzzle are straight except for a slight dip behind the tip of the nose. One nostril cuts off a corner of the cube. Indicate the other nostril by a small dark accent. Retrace over all the lines for more strength and refinement and bit by bit eliminate the cigar box forms with a kneaded eraser after they have served their purpose.

For toning the Great Dane be sure to have a clean paper stomp before dipping into the light gray chalk. Bear in mind that the dog's body is white and he is lighted from over your right shoulder. This direction of light is known as "front lighting," which makes both edges of each form have some shading. In this case the light is coming slightly from the right, so the left edges of the forms should get a bit more shading than the right.

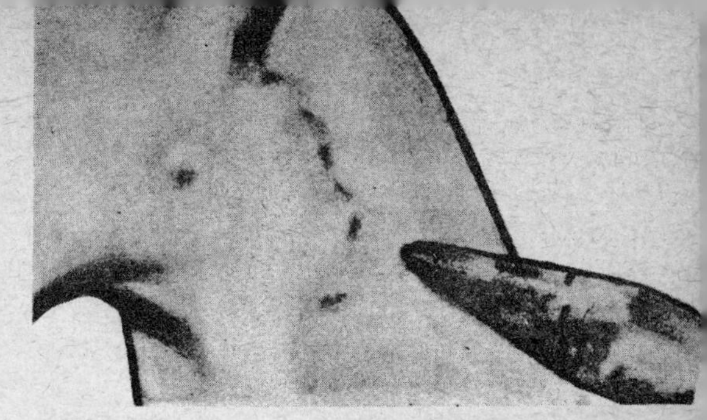

4

Erase any of the cube-like forms that are left. The dog will be white, so shading should be very faint at this point. Use the paper stomp dipped in light gray chalk dust picked up from the sandpaper pad. Let's use flat lighting here, so imagine it as coming from behind you over your right shoulder. Shade down the left side of the muzzle and the underside of lips, head and neck. Shade around the eyes and in the inside, open surfaces of the ears and also the right edge. Tone the neck and back slightly to help round out the form. Shade the iris of the eye and under the lid with the carbon pencil. Darken the front of the nose as black as possible but leave the top light gray. Use a kneaded eraser pinched to a fine point to get a highlight on the corner of the nose. With the paper dipped in gray chalk indicate trimmed whiskers and a wart on the jaw.

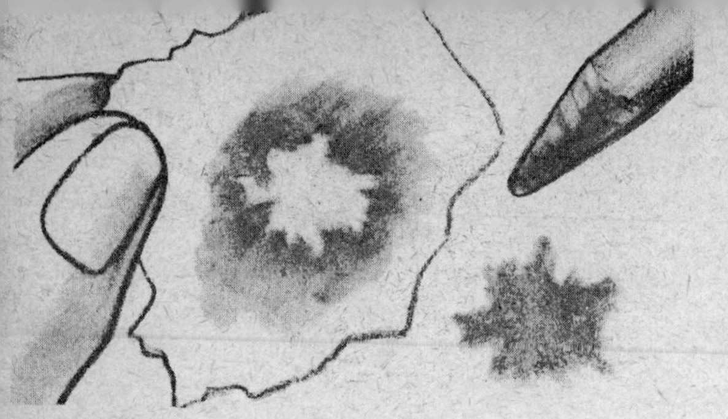

The Harlequin Great Dane has spots like torn paper or torn cloth. You can draw the spots with a pencil, but if you really want to make them look convincing, try this trick. Punch a hole in a piece of paper and then with your fingernail or tweezers tear little pieces out of the edge of the hole until it looks quite ragged. Lay the piece of torn paper down on your drawing and smudge the opening with the paper stomp dipped into black chalk dust.

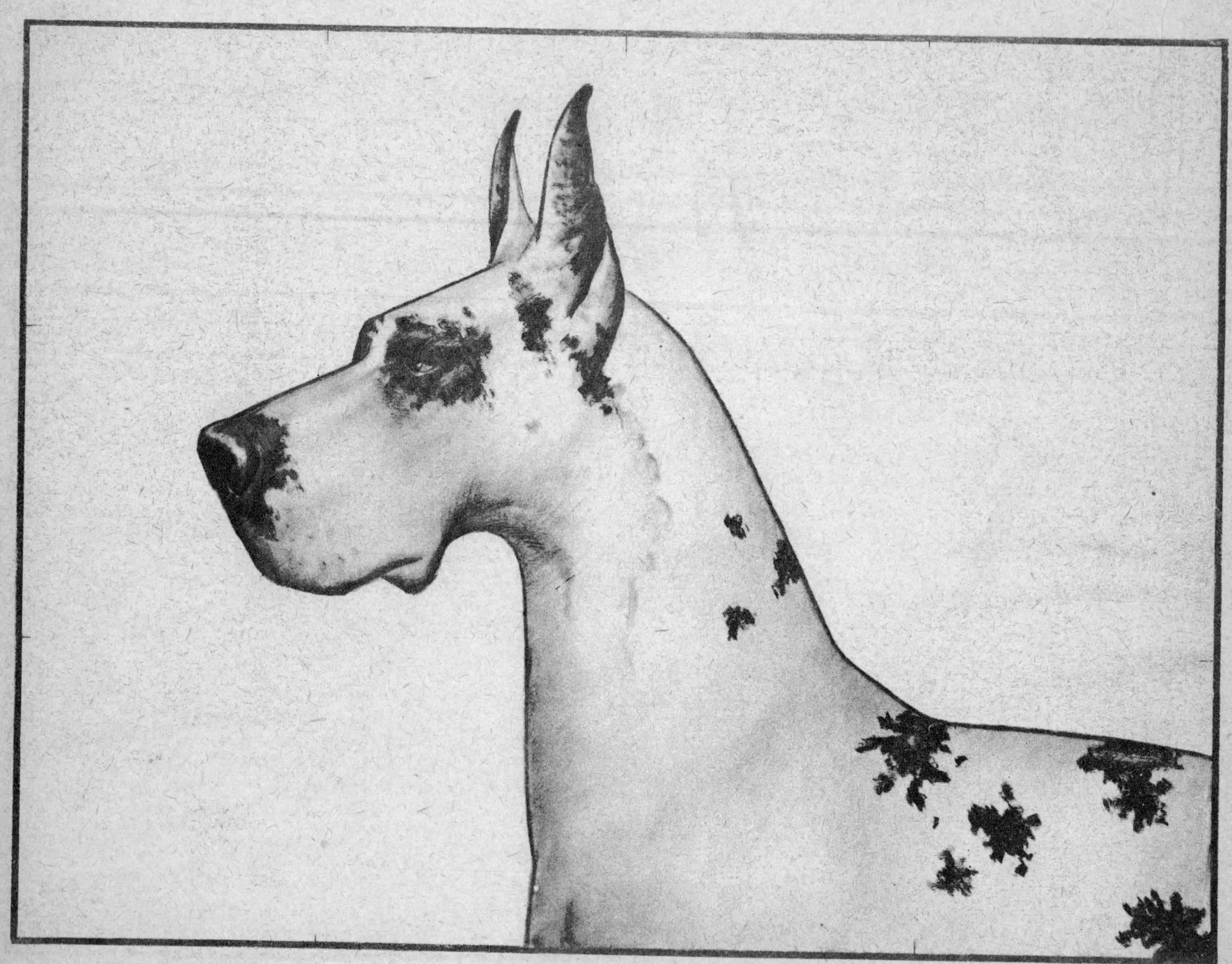

5 Spots on the Harlequin Dane are very black and shaped like torn pieces of cloth, with irregular edges, not smooth like those on a Dalmatian. Draw five of them on the back. Enlarge the dark coloration of the nostrils. Put patches over each eye. Add a little gray highlighting to the spots. Darken the inside of the ears. Spot the head but put very few spots on the neck. Darken the shading on the neck and shoulders some more to give roundness to the forms. These Harlequin spots are best drawn with the pencil by making short crisp strokes. Highlights within the spots may be made with the light gray chalk or the kneaded eraser.

The background is not quite as simple as it looks. You should have some tone movement in the background in order to create interest. By interest I mean that the over-all area should have some dark and medium dark areas blended into each other instead of being all jet black. There should be just enough tone change to suggest deep foliage background. Don't let any white or very light spots happen or they will compete in contrast with the pattern on the Great Dane.

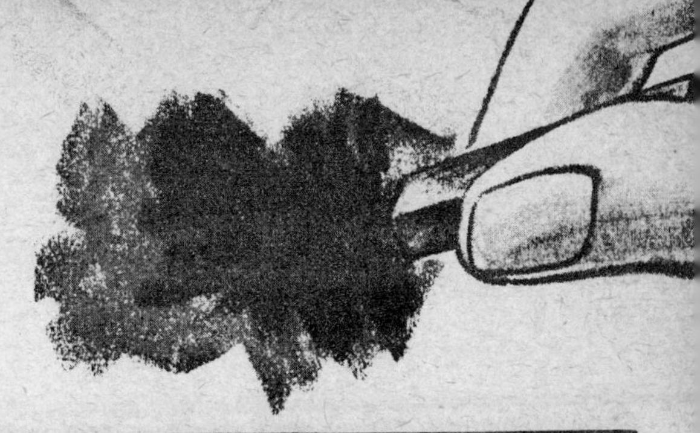

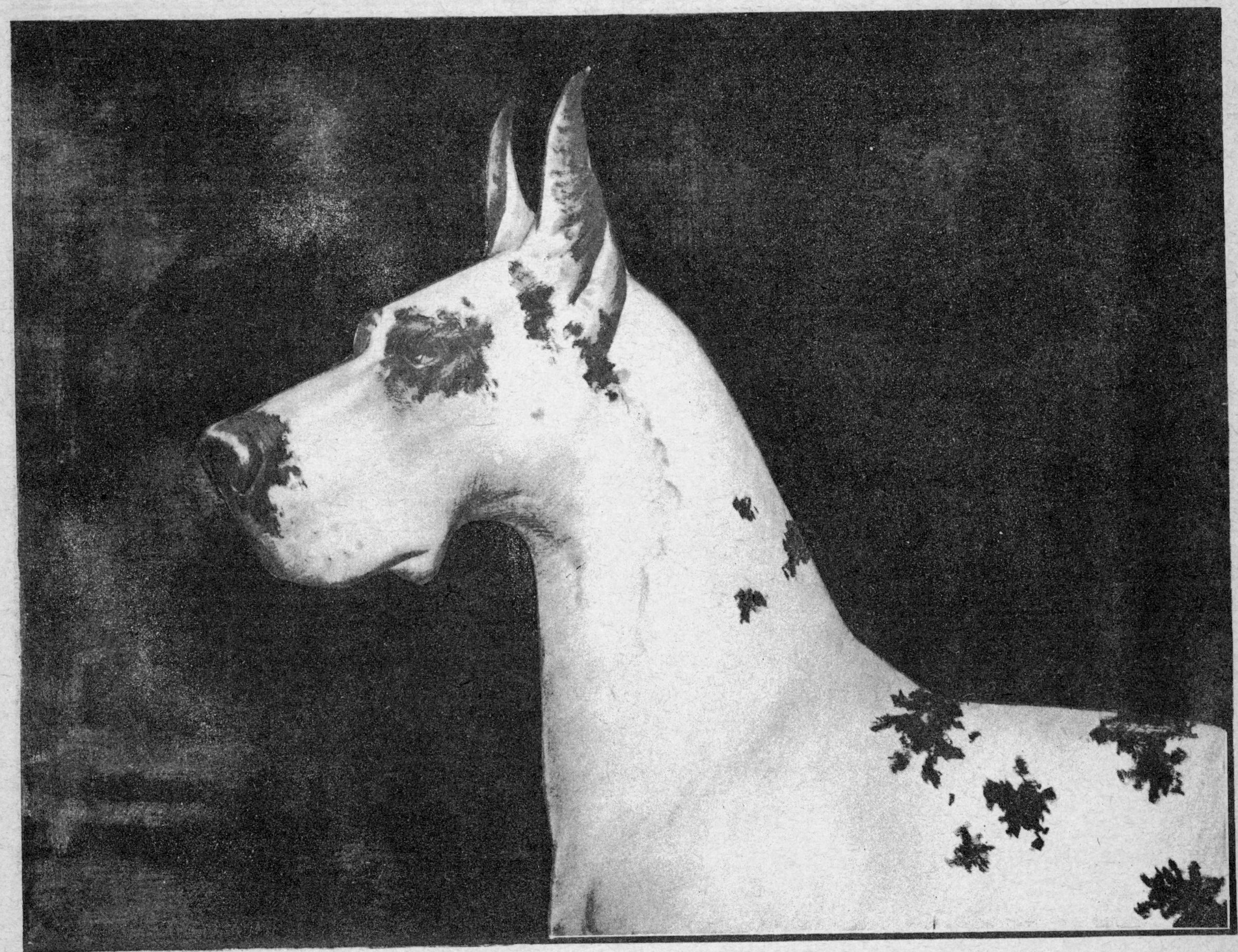

6 Tone in the background with the dark gray chalk and then go over it several times with the black chalk. Work it tightly against the edge of the dog. Stroke over and over to smooth out the background but keep some variation for light and dark patterns. Brighten the tiny highlights in the eye and on the nose by kneading your eraser and pinch it to a very fine point before picking out the light spots.

More complete information on judging the fine points of a Great Dane can be obtained in The Official Illustrated Standard of the Great Dane Club of America, Inc. I wish to acknowledge here the helpful suggestions given me by Mr. Donald E. Gauthier of Hackensack, New Jersey, who is the author of the official Great Dane manual.

COVERED BRIDGE

A scene that features depth by the use of "aerial perspective"

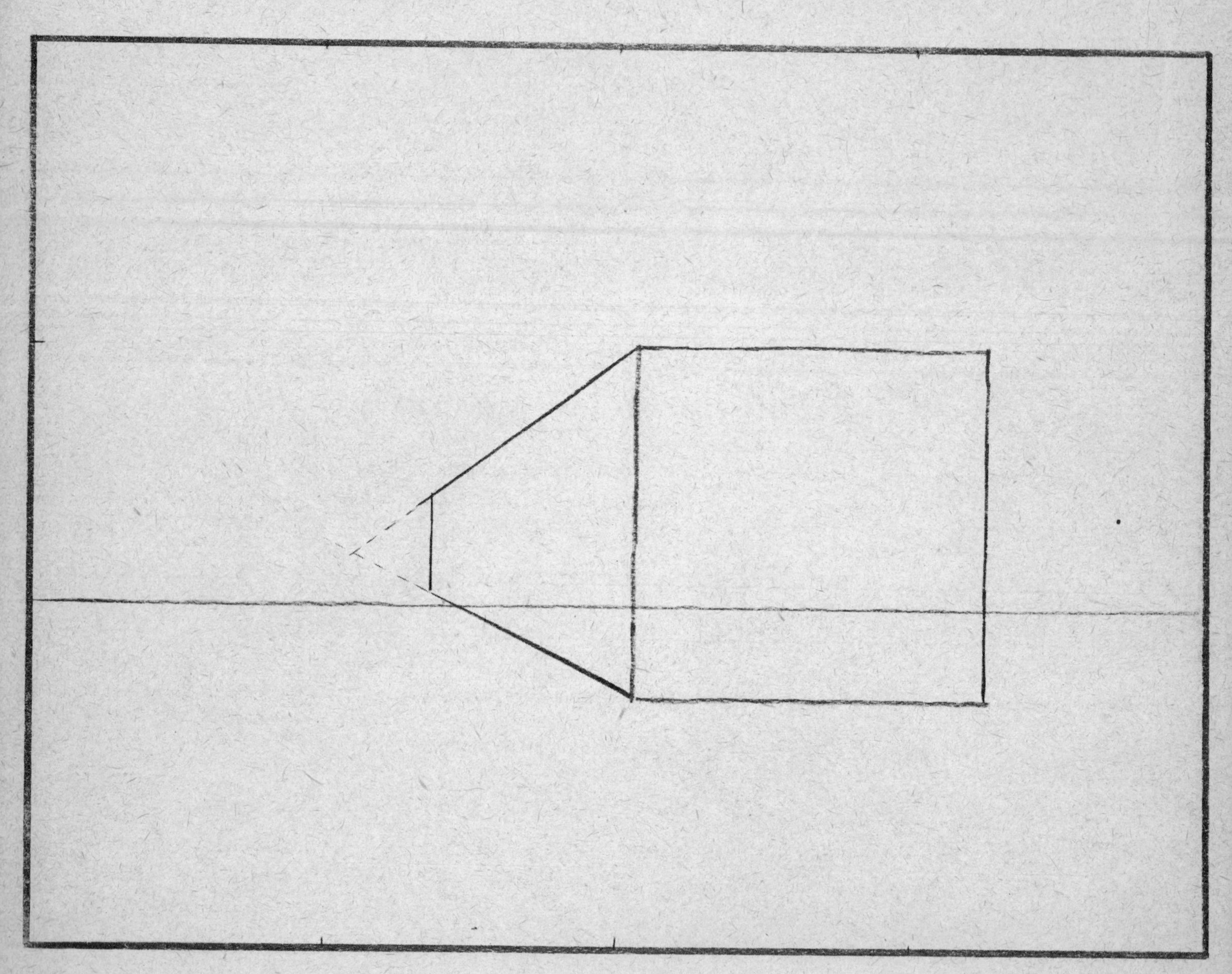

1 Draw a horizontal line for the far bank of the stream a little more than one-third up from the bottom of the paper. Draw a square in the position shown. Locate a vanishing point above the horizontal line, about one-third in from the left edge of the paper. Draw the side of a long cube from the square to the vanishing point. Erase the far end with a kneaded eraser and close the side of the long cube.

LINEAR PERSPECTIVE deals with lines that meet at a distant vanishing point and spread apart in the foreground.

SIZE PERSPECTIVE is achieved by making objects get bigger in the foreground and smaller as they go farther away.

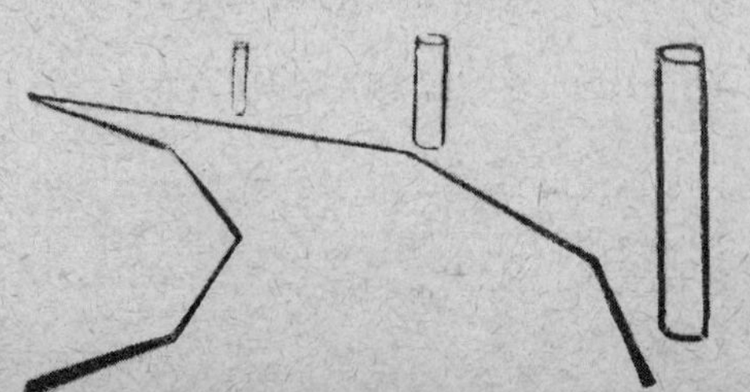

AERIAL PERSPECTIVE is caused by haze in the air, so you get the effect with tones by making distant objects lighter.

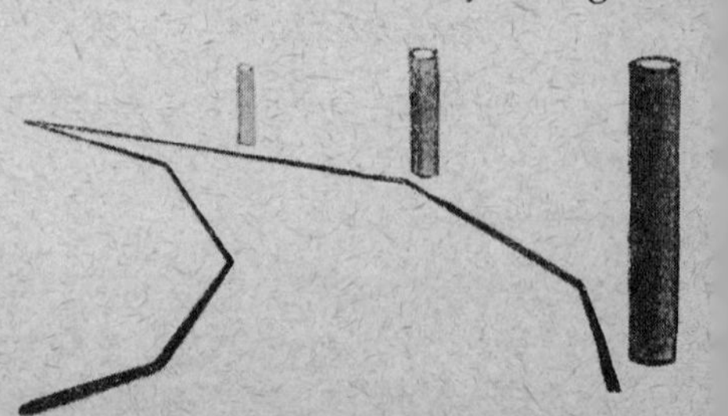

The bridge is a long cube and the pitched roof section is a half cube sliced the long way, but it is sliced diagonally through the corners. The actual roof covering is a shell that fits over the half cube. The roof shell is longer and wider than the half cube,so where it extends over the ends and sides we have an overhang called the eaves. When you draw it, make the eaves overhang but also show a little thickness to the roof edges.

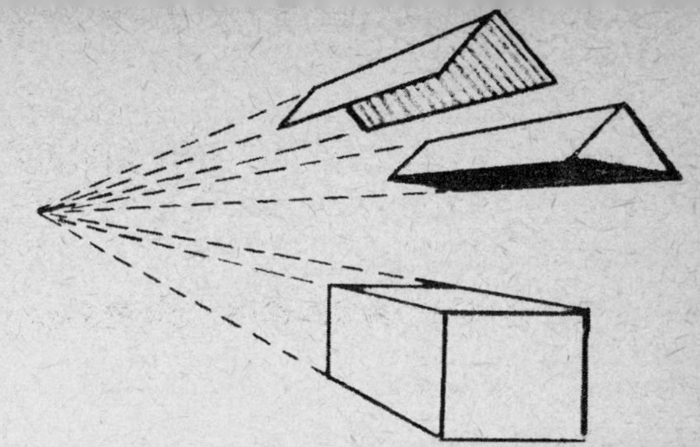

2 Draw in the top of the far bank. Add a triangular shape to the top of the cube in front and draw a roof, converging the roof lines to the original vanishing point. Be sure to make the eave seem to extend toward you, beyond the roof. Draw an opening in the bridge front and angle the top corners. Place a cube-like abutment under the far end of the bridge, resting both on the bank and into the water. Draw a long cube abutment under the center of the bridge and indicate another at the near end which will be part of a long curved cube on each side of the road for a stone wall. Draw a line inside the cube of the bridge to show the floor edge. Draw an irregular line from the left edge of the picture to the wall for the near bank and erase the line of the far bank showing through the bridge.

Masses of foliage should be suggested. Distant foliage should be very suggestive and avoid detail completely. To get the feeling of distance in treetops and shrubs be sure to use light tones. Break off a very short piece of the light gray chalk and make some crisp strokes by laying the chalk on its side. Turn it so that you are using the long sharp edge instead of the flat side. Make the strokes radiate and fan out from the center of the mass.

3 With a kneaded eraser remove the lines of the bridge from within the cube of the wall. Break off a very short piece of the light gray chalk, turn it on its corner edge and put in very light distant foliage and a suggestion of treetops. Draw a few thin lines to indicate branches and trunks. Slant strokes down to the water's edge on the far bank. With the light gray chalk on its side, tone the near bank and stroke in some light tone on the road and the top of each wall. Soften the foliage with the paper stomp or cleansing tissue. With the dark gray chalk, shade the front of the bridge, front of the abutments and the right side of the left wall. Tone the bridge front vertically for a board effect, and the floor, with dark gray chalk, horizontally. Use the flat surface of the dark gray chalk to shade under the eaves, exerting more pressure nearest the roof.

Here's where we start making good use of aerial perspective. Think of the trees back in the distance as being about a quarter of a mile away, and there is a slight haze in the air. You have put them in as suggested on the opposite page. Soften the foliage by going over lightly with stomp or cleansing tissue. Sharpen a piece of the dark gray chalk and draw the middle trees lightly. Don't give full pressure, and then shade lightly with carbon pencil

4 Tone the inside of the bridge with the very black chalk and the underside of the right eave with the carbon pencil. Draw two trees on the far bank by using the dark gray chalk, make the two trees different and taper the branches to a very thin line. Cast thin shadows from the tree down the slope of the bank. Shade the right side of trunks and branches with a carbon pencil. Remember, branches are not just pasted on. Show them firmly attached, sprouting out from each larger branch. Draw wavering upside down images for reflections in the water of the trees and abutments and cast a shadow on the road from the left wall.

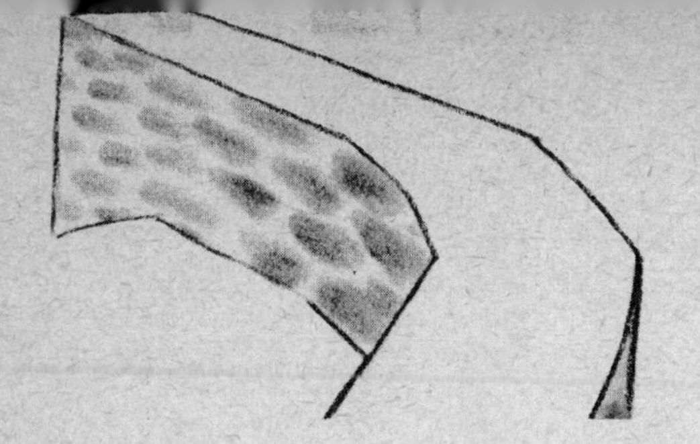

A stone wall is a long narrow cube. When it curves as it does in this composition, it is merely a long, bent cube, but never forget that it is a cube. We are looking at it from an end view, so there is considerable perspective in it. This long curved cube is actually made of many smaller irregular cubes, the stones. Be sure that you do two things in placing the stones. Make them overlap each other and make them larger as they come forward.

5 Use short pieces of both the light and dark gray chalk to shape the umbrella-like foliage of the trees in the middle distance, and a tree and bush somewhat closer on the right side of the bridge. Put shingles on the roof and vertical boards on the left side of the bridge with light gray chalk, and indicate stone work on abutments and walls with short horizontal strokes toward you. With the dark gray chalk put ruts in the road curving toward you and roughen the surface with a few cross strokes. With the carbon pencil give a dark accent to the eave along the side of the bridge and rough up the end eaves for an effect of shingles. Mark vertical crevices between the boards, darken the floor horizontally, accent the stone work of the abutments and indicate grass and reflections on the far side of the water.

Here comes the payoff in making use of the principle of Aerial Perspective. You'll only have a satisfying payoff if you have used restraint in toning the distant foliage and the middle distant trees. You can only go as black as the blackest crayon,so if you have failed to hold the distant tones light enough, you'll have little or no feeling of depth into the picture. Draw the front tree by pressing hard on the dark gray chalk and shade with the black crayon.

6 Continue the shadows of the middle distant trees onto the side of the bridge and roof. Lightly outline the stone work on the walls with irregular ellipses, being sure to keep the top stones flat. Cast a shadow from the close end of the bridge over the end of the left wall, the road and up and over the right wall, making sure that it follows the contours of the ruts. Put the texture of grain and knots in the bridge end. Draw a big tree in the foreground with a short piece of dark gray chalk flat on its side, massing in the trunk and three large branches. With the very black chalk shade the right side of the cylinder form of the trunk and branches, and mass in foliage, leaving some open spaces. Doodle around the clusters, define leaf shapes at the edges with the carbon pencil and sketch in blades of grass. Cast a shadow up the slope, two shadows over the left wall, drop to the road, into and over the ruts and over the right wall. Add patches of leafy shadows. Outline some stones on the shaded side of the wall with the carbon pencil.

WHISTLE STOP

An example of "linear perspective" in depicting a prairie town

1 Draw a horizon line about a third of the way up from the bottom of the paper. Locate a vanishing point about a quarter of the way in from the left, and from it draw the curving lines of a track. See Page 9 for perspective in tracks. To give the tracks thickness and height, make long cubes of them by drawing three lines for each. Draw the ties with a ruler, perfectly horizontal, close and narrow in the distance, wider and darker as they come forward, and extend them beyond the track on each side.

For the train, draw a circle above the tracks and converge lines from it to the vanishing point. For the boiler, cut off a section to make a foreshortened cylinder and draw a foreshortened cube behind the boiler for the engine cab.

Because of the intense perspective in this picture of the train it is not necessary to draw exact and accurate wheels. But when you use suggestion in a picture, it is very important to have exact knowledge in order to make your suggestion convincing. The coaches and coal car of a train have smaller wheels than the drive wheels of the engine. The wheels are vertical ellipses like the exercises on page two.

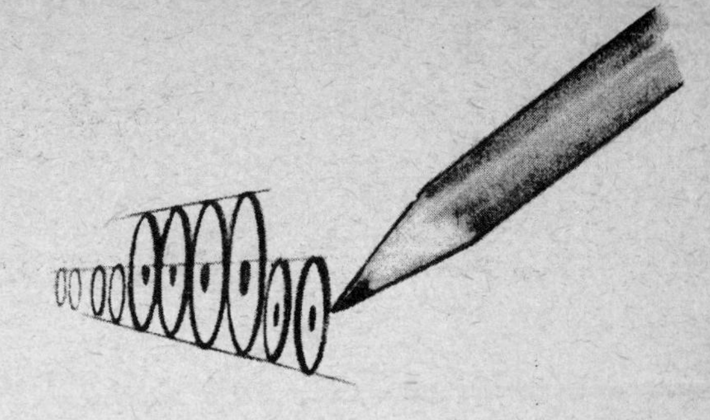

2 Draw two flattened cone forms of grain, light them from the upper left, shade them on the right with the paper stomp. Draw a cube-like beam under the front of the boiler, and cow catcher, which is another cube-like form extending forward. Shade the front of the boiler with a carbon pencil, leaving a white circle for the headlight. Shade the right side of the cow catcher and the front of the cabin behind the boiler. Draw vertical lines to separate the cars and narrow elliptical wheels beneath, touching the track. Draw two cylinders for pistons and add the smoke stack and other attachments. Pencil five vertical lines for poles, larger and bolder as they come forward. Add cross bars to each pole. Indicate spike heads holding the tracks to the ties and shade the inside of the rails.

Let's first look at the drawing at the bottom of the page. Here we used a different vanishing point for the buildings from the one used for the train, yet they are on the same horizon line. The reason is that the train tracks curve. Now the telegraph poles. After you have established the poles and cross bars in line, sharpen your light gray chalk and put in the tone at the left of the poles and above cross bars, leaving the shading at right and below.

3 Locate a vanishing point in the middle of the horizon line and use it to draw cube forms at the right and left of the picture. Eliminate the base of the closest pole from inside the cube with a kneaded eraser. Draw a double horizontal line for a roadway crossing the tracks. Thicken poles with light gray tone on the left of each and thicken the cross bars. Draw the curb of a platform with a double line for height. With the light gray chalk draw an embankment line at the right. Use short, curved strokes without lifting your chalk from the paper.

Below you will see how the ellipses at the tops and bottoms of the grain storage bins would look if you could see through them. These bins may also have their own vanishing point on the same horizon line as the other objects in the picture, or you may use the same vanishing point that was used for the buildings. The sketch at the right shows a different kind of rain barrel plus a bag of mail that has been tossed off at the whistle stop.

4 Roof the cubes with triangular shapes. Overhang the left one with an eave and draw a cupola on top. Draw double lines to give thickness to the edges of the roofs. Set a cylinder form at the corner for an old-fashioned water barrel, used in case of fire. Draw a cone shaped lid on it. Line up seven cylinders for grain storage bins at the right, using the vanishing point in the middle of the horizon to give them the right perspective.

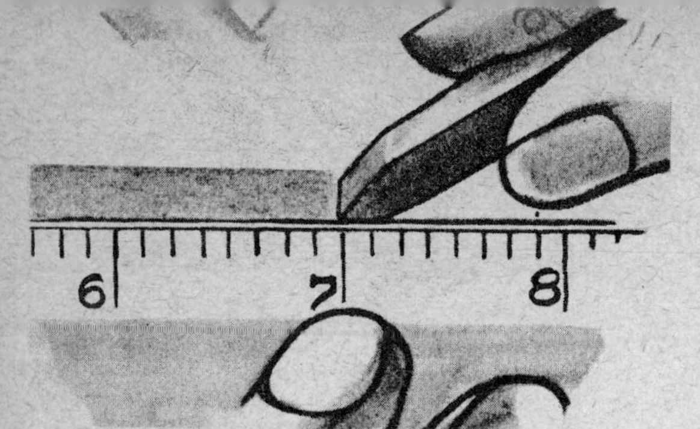

Who says it's wrong to use a ruler to make a straight line? Every professional artist uses easy ways to help him get his job done better and more quickly. So why shouldn't you? No surgeon would purposely operate with a table knife unless he is a show-off. Let's get straight about using a ruler, compass, T square, enlarger, kneaded eraser, crayons, or any means that will help make the finished drawing better. Use a ruler to draw the boards on the old station.

5

Draw the edge of a signboard on the side of the depot. Shade the front of the depot and the right side of the grain elevator across the tracks with the dark gray chalk. With the light gray chalk tone the left side of the depot, leaving the sign white, and tone and shade the cylinder forms of the rain barrel and storage bins. Tone the top of the platform and ground across the tracks with the light gray chalk, using horizontal strokes. Suggest a lightning rod on the cupola and a window in the engine cabin. Tone the cylinder form of the boiler from light gray to dark gray beneath. Shade the platform edge with the carbon pencil.

Did you know that many professional artists use a simple and quick method for making a slightly curved line when they don't use a French curve? Just raise up the edge of your ruler by placing your finger or thumb under the edge. Put your pencil against the edge and as you draw a line gradually change the angle of the pencil. If you do it in a single rhythmic stroke, you get a curved line such as you need for the telegraph wires.

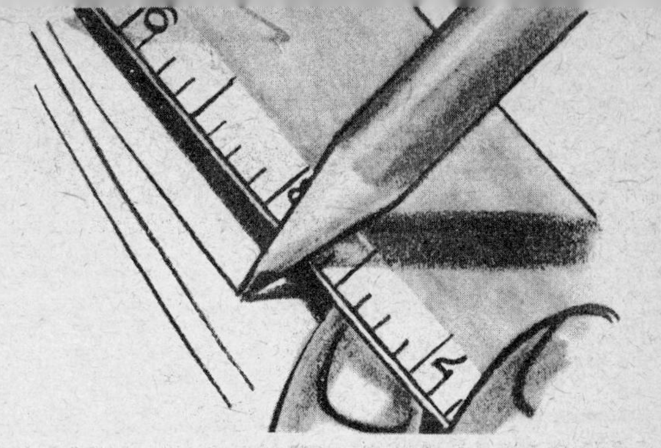

6 Draw doors, windows and clapboards with a ruler. Texture the roofs, the foreground ties and the platform with short pencil strokes. Draw the grass with short strokes. Draw the slats in the left side of the cow catcher. Subdue the headlight. Indicate engine rods with the carbon pencil. Tone the engine cabin and cars, with the paper stomp. Put in a crossing post, insulators and wires on the poles and dots for sparrows. Shade under the depot eaves with the carbon pencil, add curved brackets and other trim and put an eave on the grain elevator. Letter the sign. Indicate a silhouetted figure against the depot wall. Put hoops around the water barrel and cast a shadow from it. Cast a shadow from the depot to the grass, carefully following every contour. Cast a shadow from the engine and smoke shadows on the bins. Draw the pigeons. Doodle the smoke in circles with the dark gray chalk. Use the paper stomp, a tissue or your finger to smudge it.

GOOD NEIGHBOR

This simple portrait demonstrates the use of the basic forms

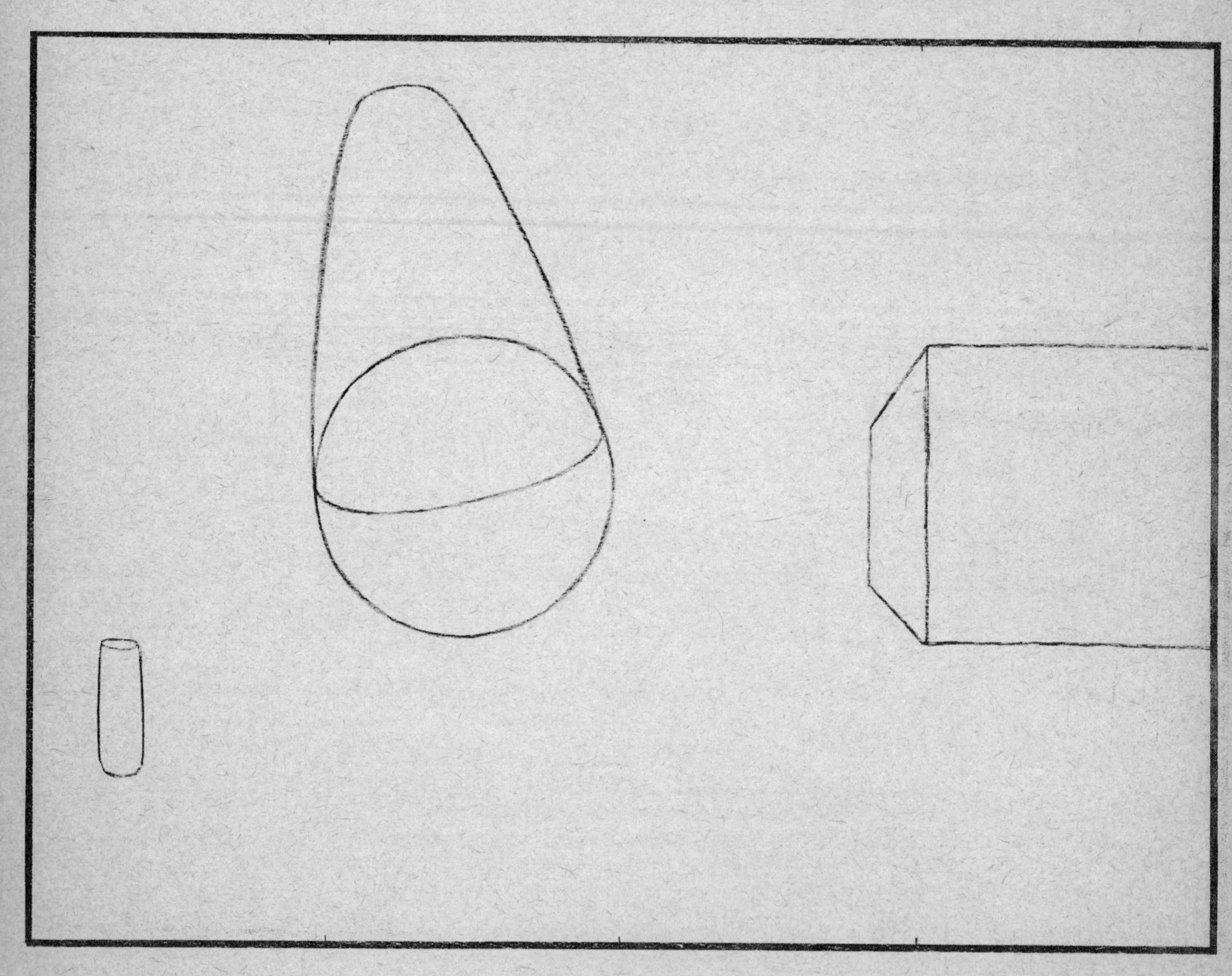

1 We begin our Mexican scene by drawing a cube, ball, cone and cylinder in the positions shown, the cone placed over the ball and with rounded tip. See that the cone is properly slanted. Draw the base of the cube about even with the bottom of the ball form. Keep the cylinder very small in comparison to the other forms.

Nothing takes the place of freehand practice in making sketches,so practice ellipses shown on page 3 until you can do them freehand, then when you make your finished drawing, you can use a trick to help get a better result. Fold a piece of paper once, then fold it the other way. Cut a curved snip from it as shown but make the snip one half as long and wide as the ellipse you want. Then trace around it as shown below.

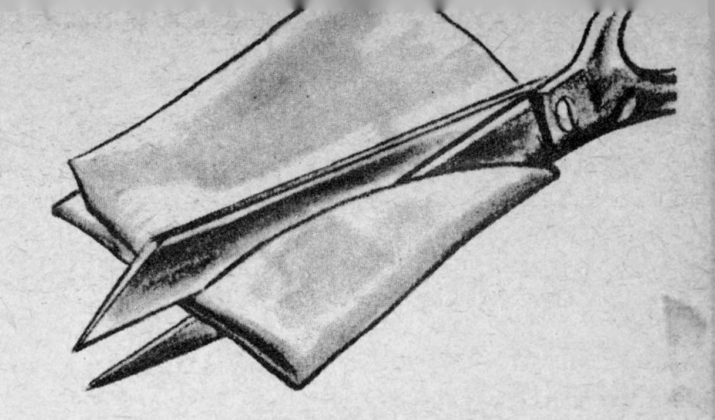

2 Keeping your strokes very light, draw an oval, overlapping the ball form for the lower part of the boy's face. Draw smaller ovals for his cheeks and chin, and a small circle for his nose. Indicate the edge of his neck with a curved line and drape the shoulders with rhythmic strokes to indicate the soft folds of a blanket. Draw a horizon line below the center of the page, stopping at the cube, to indicate the point at which the desert floor meets mountains in the background. Draw a large ellipse for the top of the hat brim, and curve the under edge like a bowl.

Learn to think clear around an object so that when you see it from one view you can stretch your mind around behind it or from the side and visualize how it would look. A sculptor learns about three dimensional vision because he is actually working with height, width, and thickness. He must turn the clay around constantly and work from every angle. If you practice doing this in making drawings, they will have a much greater feeling of being real and three dimensional.

3 Draw a cone-like mountain behind the hat and cube, and with a short piece of gray chalk tone in the sky, blending with the paper stomp. Draw almond-shaped eyes, slightly slanted, but open wide, making the iris large and dark with a soft highlight. With a pinched kneaded eraser eliminate most of the light lines inside the face and hat. Keep the curve of the circles at the corners of the mouth to indicate bulged cheeks, and go over the outline of the whole face, cheeks and chin, using the carbon pencil to connect them with a rhythmic outline. Erase any sketchy lines left. Draw a rounded tip of nose and a smiling mouth. Add a ball form to the cylinder top and an oval form beside it for a cactus.

In drawing an eye it is important to think of basic forms. The eye is a ball set deeply into the eye socket, and you are only seeing the front part of the ball that bulges forward. The eye lids are flaps made of muscle tissue that slide over the front surface of the ball. Remember, too, that the eyelids themslves are thick and not just paper-thin forms. When the eye is open the upper lid slides back under the bone and leaves a crevice.

4 Tone the face with the paper stomp dipped in powdered light gray chalk. Use the other end of the stomp, dipped in dark gray, to shade the side of the face, nose, cheeks, chin and neck. Tone the cylinder form of the cactus with light and dark gray chalk and shade it. Erase a highlight on the tip of the nose. With the carbon pencil accent the outlines of the eyes, nose, mouth, face and neck. Dip the paper stomp in light gray chalk and streak in soft tones over the desert floor.

Desert plants such as the tumbleweed, the pancake cactus, cholla, beavertail and barrel cactus have fascinating forms that add relief to the otherwise barren waste of open spaces. These plants have adapted themselves to the arid climate so that they can go for months on end without rain. In the rainy months of January and February they bloom and flower beautifully. Learn to represent their forms so that you can make ready use of them in any picture you might attempt of the great Southwest.

5 With the dark gray chalk shade the left side of the hat crown, the left and under side of the brim, inside the brim on the right, and left side of the cube-like building. With the light gray chalk tone the boy's blanket, cast a shadow from the building and draw in shrubs and tumbleweeds. Draw the texture of lines and needles on the cactus, and cast a shadow from it, with the carbon pencil.

Texture is the final touch you put on objects to make them look real. For example, the texture of the boy's hat makes it look as though it is woven of straw instead of being made of paper or tin. The adobe houses of the Southwest also have texture, and as they age, they develop more texture than when they are new. If you'd like to add more character to your drawing, try showing the stucco fallen away from the adobe bricks on the building.

6 With the carbon pencil, cast a shadow on the face, curving over the ball form of the cheek, cylinder form of the nose and the ball form of the other cheek. Lay in tone carefully with pencil strokes side by side and some cross hatch in the other direction. Keep the pencil sharply pointed to texture the hat. Pencil designs on the blanket and pencil in the hair very black. Cross hatch the neck, cast a shadow from the nose, and shade the cheek and jaw. Draw a light gray door in the building, and two ladder shadows, then the ladder. With the carbon pencil draw rafter poles and their shadows and shade the sides of the ladder and rungs. Outline the door, put on cross-battens, and give the building a window. Indicate a figure on the ground and another on the roof. Draw a small cactus in the right foreground. Accent the sagebrush and tumbleweed. Give the building shadow some texture. Tone the mountain with the paper stomp dipped in light gray chalk.

THE HUMAN FIGURE *in action and expression*

Figure illustration is a special field for the advanced student. If you want to draw and paint people, you must make a study of human actions. But your study must go deeper than that. You should know clearly what idea causes the action. So if you are going to draw a human being doing something, be sure that you know what idea is in his head making him act that way. For example, on this page we have some stick figures of people in various actions. At the left, the child, the man, and the woman are just standing there like dummies being measured. The child is five and one half heads high; the woman is seven and a half heads high, and the man is eight heads high. One of the figures is measuring the height of a head. Another one is counting the heads. Others are jumping, running, walking, dancing, etcetera. But each one has an idea that makes him act the way he does. You should practice drawing hundreds of stick figures in action and always have an idea behind the action.

In landscape or still-life drawing you don't have to figure out what a tree or a hill or a pumpkin is thinking.

The eyes, eyebrows, and mouth express feelings and thoughts by their shapes and positions.

Woe is me! *You brute!* *What you said!* *How charming!*

The stick figure does not represent the bone skeleton, but it is the central line through each mass of form,

They just sit there looking like a cylinder or a cone or a ball with all the trimmings. Your action figures must also be made to look like cylinder, ball, cone, and cube forms or they won't look real. After you have sketched a stick figure, give it form by making the chest and pelvis like tapered cubes and make the limbs and body like tapered cylinders. Use a ball form at each joint. After you have clothed the stick figure with chunks of form, just slide your sketch under a sheet of paper that you can see through and draw the smooth lines of the figure on the top sheet.

These FACIAL EXPRESSIONS are the actions of eyes, eyebrows, and mouth, caused by thoughts and emotions. Do a little acting on your own in front of a mirror and look for these principles. When the top line of the eye is straight and you see white below the pupil, it makes you look stern. If the brows point up in the center of the forehead and down at the outside ends, you look sad or fatigued or sick. If the brows push down at the center, you look angry. When you see white above the pupil and the lower lid is straight and the brows are raised, you look surprised. If the outside corners of the eyes slant up, you look pleased. Eyebrows raised and eyelids brought down over the eyes, you look supercilious. One brow raised and the other lowered, you look quizzical.

as if a wire were run through dead center of each chunk of matter. The stick figure is the essence of action.

VARIATIONS OF THE BASIC FORMS

The secret of being able to sketch objects and people in outline is found in the four basic forms. Develop the habit of looking for variations and combinations of these forms and your sketches will have mass and thickness instead of looking flat. A simple example of combinations of forms is the banana. It is made of a curved cylinder that tapers to a cone at each end. But it also has some of the surface planes and edges of the cube. So instead of blending it softly round, as you would a cone or a cylinder, you draw lines to make the edges of flat planes on it. You tone each plane a different flat value to get the angular surface of a banana. Then your drawing of the banana looks very real because you saw it as cylinder, cone, and cube forms.

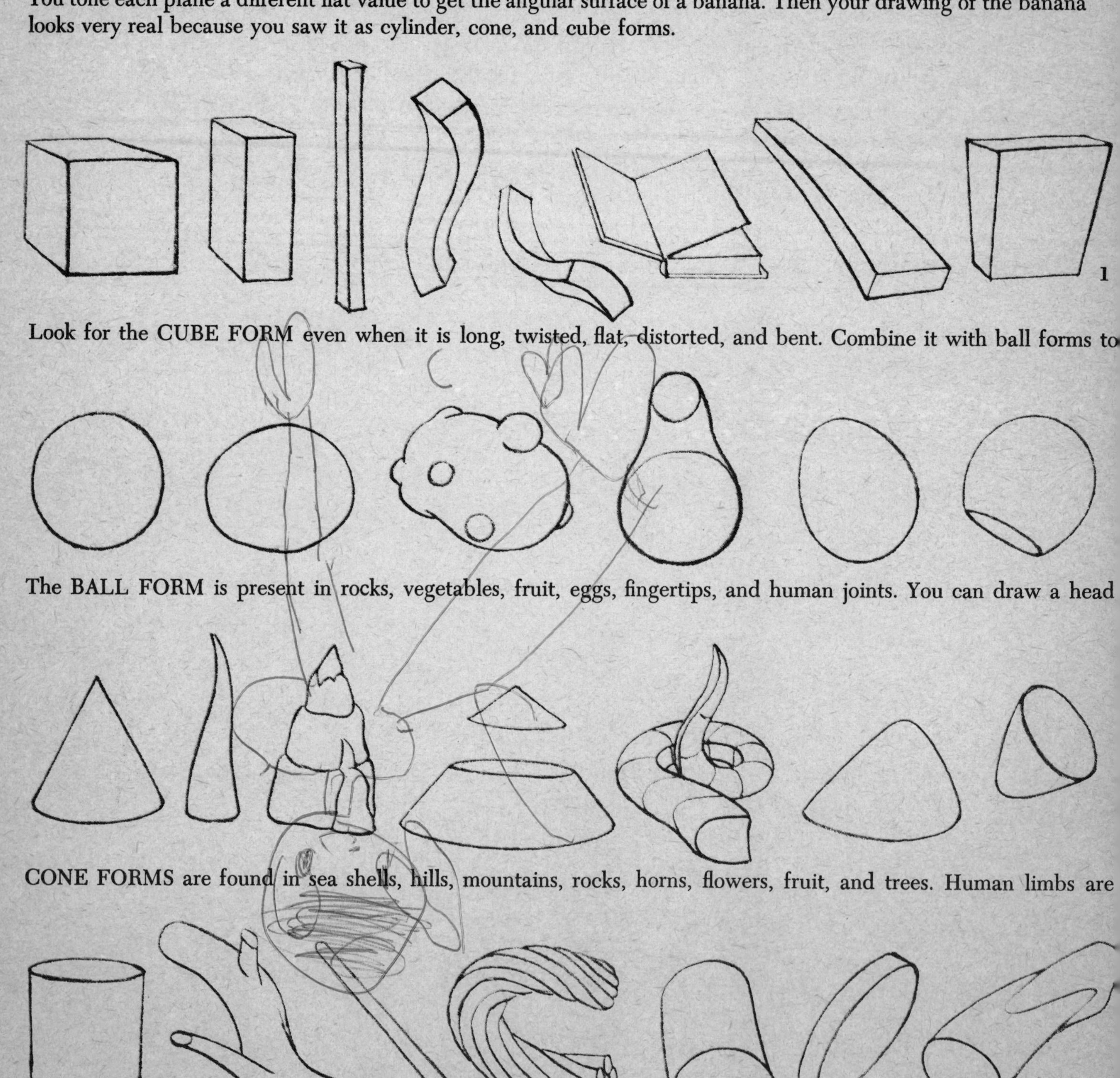

Look for the CUBE FORM even when it is long, twisted, flat, distorted, and bent. Combine it with ball forms to

The BALL FORM is present in rocks, vegetables, fruit, eggs, fingertips, and human joints. You can draw a head

CONE FORMS are found in sea shells, hills, mountains, rocks, horns, flowers, fruit, and trees. Human limbs are

The CYLINDER FORMS in nature always taper and are bent or twisted. In anatomy they appear oval-shaped

and how they combine to build the human figure

Now take a look at your own hand. Think of the mass of the palm as being a flattened cube, not paper-thin but medium-thick. Your fingers and thumb and wrist are tapered cylinders, and your fingertips each end as a half-ball form. The base of your thumb is an egg-shaped ball form growing out of the corner of the cubelike palm. Look at the lines in the palm of your hand and realize that they are not lines at all. They are valleys where two or more forms meet. In drawing, you suggest the valleys with a line, but be sure to shade each form and let your shading stop at the edge of each valley. Latch on to this way of thinking when you look at anything, and you'll soon be drawing convincing pictures that will amaze you.

make pelvis and hips.

with the ball and cone.

combined cone and cylinder forms.

when seen in cross section.

ON THE NEXT TWO PAGES YOU WILL SEE HOW TO GET PERSPECTIVE BY FORESHORTENING.

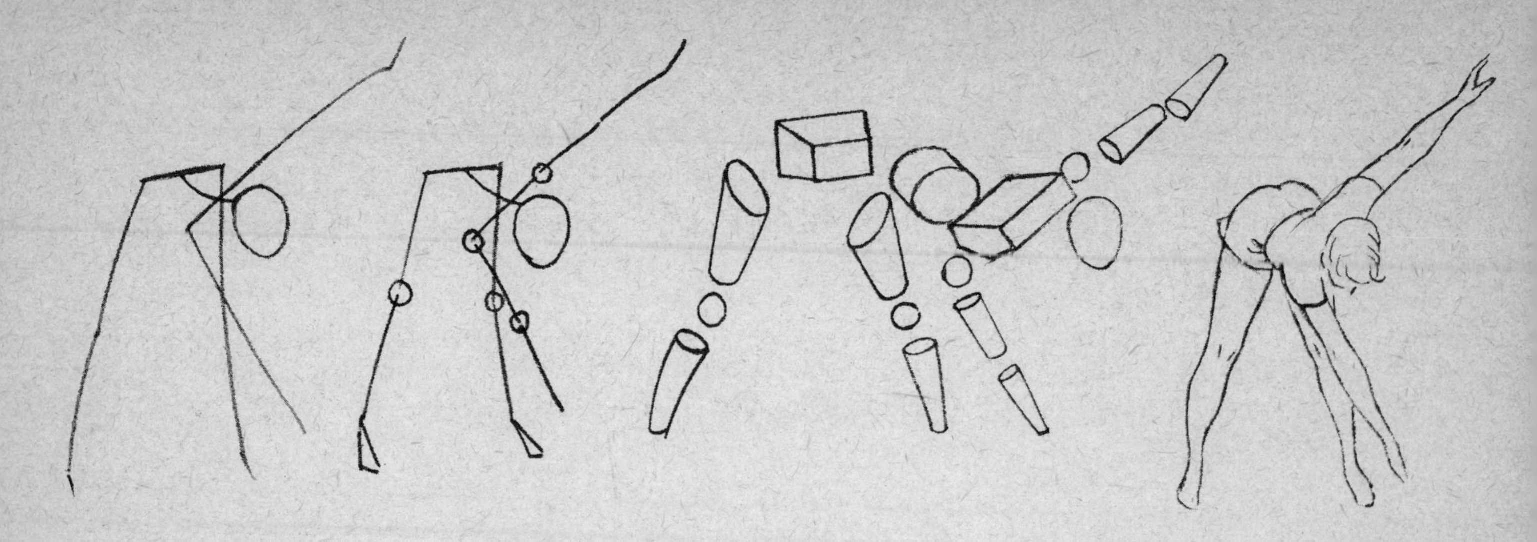

FORESHORTENED CUBES and CYLINDERS

What does foreshorten mean? The best example I can give you is to look at the end of a log, and as you look down the side of it toward the other end you will notice that the log is considerably shortened in appearance. Also look at the row of distorted cube forms on pages 56 and 57. Notice how the plank is foreshortened. Then look at the wedge-shaped cube to the right of it. This one is not foreshortened, but as you look at the next four at the right of it you'll see how each step is more foreshortened than the one just before it. Something else has been done to it in steps 2 and 4 and 5. In step 2 the left side of it has been squeezed down and the right side of it has been stretched. In step 3 it has only been turned farther around in space, so the broad surface became foreshortened. In step 4 it is turned farther, but also it has been twisted so that the top corner that will be the fighter's right shoulder has been pushed forward and the left shoulder is pulled back. The lower part of the cube that comes at the fighter's waist has not been changed. In step 5 the upper left surface has been sliced off to make the front plane of the man's chest. When you practice this kind of foreshortening you'll get remarkable perspective in your figure drawings. Always block in the chest and pelvis with cubelike forms over your stick figure.

Now look at the figures on these pages. Notice how the torso of the slim woman at the top of the page is a foreshortened cylinder. The legs and forearm of the figure below are foreshortened cylinders. The plump woman is also a group of cylinders, but they have become ball-like, so her forms are a combination of ball and cylinder.

will give your figures the kind of perspective they need

Now try your hand at it and watch your progress over a period of time. Nothing pays off more than constant practice. Actually talent is a rather misleading word. Talent means that you have a strong desire that keeps you everlastingly at your work. I have watched the progress of many a person who couldn't draw at all, and I have seen them gradually become good at drawing and painting as they repeatedly applied the principles shown you on these pages. Frankly, everyone who can draw well has practiced constantly. This has been so true in my own family. My wife and son and daughter and myself have never attended art school, but by making an attempt at sketching every day, each one of us has improved week by week. The figure drawings on these six pages were done by my wife, Mary Jo, and I literally picked them out of the wastebasket. They were made on scraps of paper, grocery lists, and menus. I have used them purposely as an example of what can be done by one who applies the principles of building pictures out of the basic forms. I have taken each drawing apart to show how her mind grasped each form and action from stick figure to finished result. The drawing of the boxers is a particularly good example because she drew it in ink and couldn't erase the stick figures or the cubelike construction of the chest and shoulders. It's all right there in the drawing. Sometimes she consciously applies the basic principles, but most of the time now it is subconscious. The method, when well learned, becomes automatic after frequent practice. You should be no exception. It can happen to you too.

YOUR "IDEA FILE"

Your *Idea File* is like an artist's sketch book. The artist gathers interesting pieces of nature and saves them. Later when he pages through his sketches *ideas* come easily as he begins to combine various objects that seem related. He puts them together into a real picture that looks as though the whole scene had happened the moment he came along. Actually, most good pictures are created by imagination and the putting together of things that could have happened just that way.

You should sketch objects from nature, too, and start an *Idea File* of your own. Also clip pictures from magazines and newspapers and build up your supply of *idea material*.

When you look at any object *always* try to analyze whether it is made of a CUBE or BALL, a CONE or a CYLINDER. Most objects are made of combinations of the four basic forms. Bear in mind, too, that you seldom find perfectly symmetrical CUBE, BALL, CONE or CYLINDER forms in nature. Most often they are distorted and bent or lopsided compared to the mechanical ones we can draw. These variations are what make the forms interesting and pleasant instead of stiff and mechanical.

Study the drawings on this page and on the last page of the book to see how I have looked for combinations and variations of the basic forms. They are revealed in the cut apart and exploded views at the left of each drawing. The reason you should do it, too, is so that you can draw objects that appear to have thickness. Also, when you know what kind of basic forms make up the object, you know where to put the shading after you have decided the direction of the light.

OUTLINE WITHOUT THEIR TEXTURES, THEN ADD TONE, SHADING, CAST SHADOWS AND FINAL TEXTURE

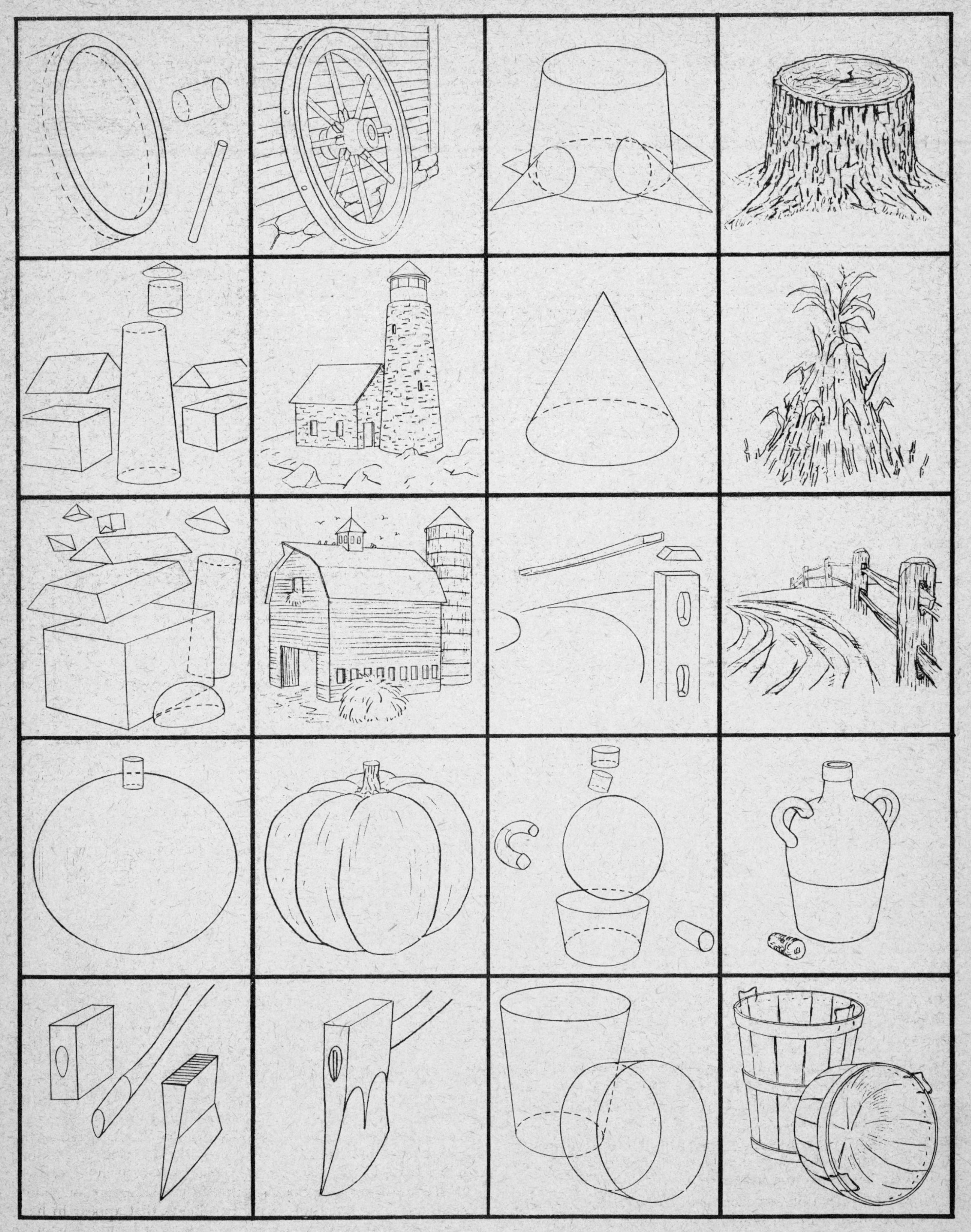

On the next two pages you will discover the fun you can have in making your own picture compositions by using drawings from this "Idea File"

YOUR PICTURE PUZZLE TEST

What is the purpose of these

FIRST • *To show you how to combine the familiar objects from your "Idea File".*

Your next job is to make new compositions by putting together the pictures of objects so they make real pictures like these. See how many new combinations you can make. Add some of your own ideas. For example, combine the swan and a frog. You can find a picture of a frog in a natural history book. Combine the cowboy and the lady, but be sure that the cowboy's head is small enough to keep him back in the distance. You'll be making use of *size perspective* when you do that. NOW START your imagination to work and see what interesting pictures you can make.

WHY would you use two different tools to complete the drawing of the fish? Study paragraph 7 on page 5 and page 7, then look at the picture of the sailfish on page 64. The fish and the fisherman need something added to them that you will find in paragraphs 4 and 5 on page 4, page 5, and page 7. Study page 2 for the tools to use.

WHAT three treatments are missing in this composition? Your answers will be found on pages 3, 4 and 5 in paragraphs 4, 5 and 6. From which direction will you light the barn, the silo, the house and the fence if you light and shade the rooster as he is on page 64? Will the cast shadows of the fence fall to the right or to the left?

HOW would you complete this drawing in the background? You could draw the edge of a hill, a tree and a shed without cluttering the composition. Would you treat the background bold or light? See the paragraphs on aerial perspective on pages 42, 45 and 47. You'll find how to draw the log, sawbuck, stump, axe and turkey in the idea file on pages 60, 61 and 64. Then add tone, shading and texture.

WHERE does this picture need something mentioned in paragraphs 4, 5 and 6 on page 7? You can learn something about treating the rocks in paragraph 7 on page 5. When you are ready to pick out some highlights on the fish and the lobster take a look at the top of page 21. The fish is darker above and lighter on its under side because of its natural color and not because of the direction of light.

unfinished compositions?

SECOND • *To test your observation by figuring out what is missing in each picture.*

These compositions are "think problems" to help you prove whether or not you have learned the lessons in the NEW ART BOOK. These pictures are incomplete. Some are just drawn in outline, others have outline and TONE in parts of them. Several of the drawings have TEXTURE and in a few cases you will find that the SHADING is also added. In only one of the drawings have I added CAST SHADOWS. Use the enlarging method on page 8 to make your drawings either 6 x 8 or 9 x 12 inches in size. When you have your sketch made in outline, add TONE, SHADING, CAST SHADOWS and TEXTURE.

You learn to exercise your logical imagination by putting together related objects. Your picture has harmony of subject matter when you combine objects that seem to belong together in the same setting. This kind of art is called REALISM.

When you put together unrelated objects, you get another kind of art depending on *how* you put them together. For example, you might combine the fish and the dinner bell. If you drew the fish flying over the dinner bell, your picture would be called SURREALISM which means beyond realism. But if you drew the fish on a platter appetizingly cooked with steaming vegetables and combined it with the dinner bell, it would be called SYMBOLISM. Each of the ISMS has its place in the world of art, but the purpose of these lessons is to help you, the beginner, enjoy drawing REAL PICTURES.

WHEN a picture like the one above looks finished but some of the objects seem to lack substance, what do they need? In paragraph 4 on page 7 you will find what is needed on the corn shocks, pumpkin, wheel, baskets and jug. The corn shocks and pumpkin have something that the wheel, baskets and jug don't have. Find your answer in paragraph 5 on pages 4 and 7.

WHERE would you put three large areas of tone if you wanted to make the beach, the rocks and the buildings stand out white in contrast? The snow scene on page 29 should give you one clue. Would you make all three areas of tone the same value? Read page 8 again. Buildings, rocks and boat will have more form if you follow paragraph 5 on pages 4 and 7.

WHAT direction of light is indicated in this picture? On page 64 you'll find the head of the man and the horse. Which one is lighted correctly to use in this composition? What must you do in lighting and shading the other one to make it belong in the same picture? Study the basic forms at the left of the pictures on page 64 and then look at paragraph 5 on pages 4 and 7.

WHY would you tone the field and corn shocks very lightly in this composition? Your answer will be found on pages 42, 45 and 47. To which side of the corn shocks and fence posts would you cast the shadows on the ground? On which side of the fence posts would you put shading? Just study the light and shade on the bell and post and you have your answer.

Here are some more advanced pictures for your "Idea File"

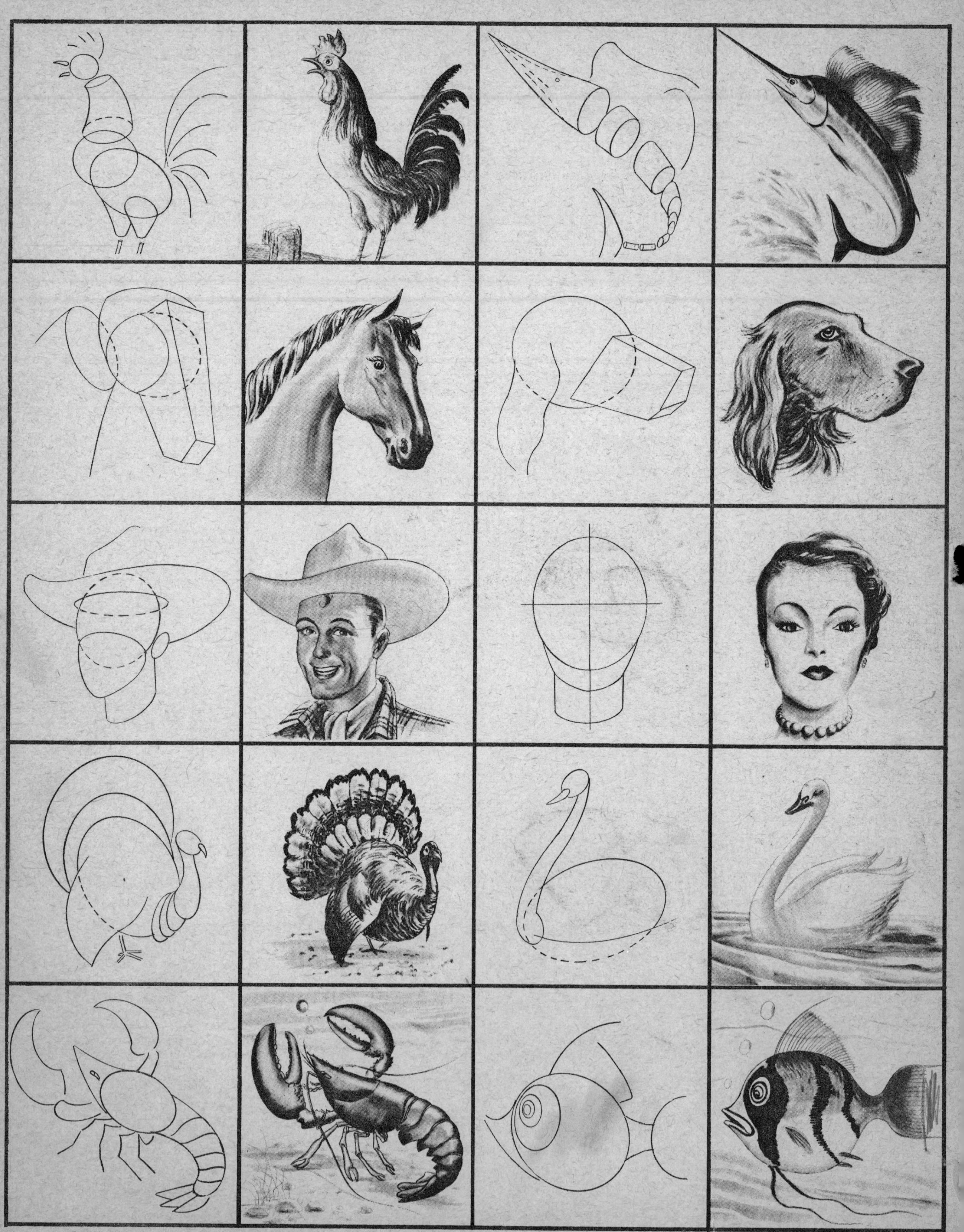